DEVELOP...IN
THE MIDDLE YEARS

Open University Press

English, Language, and Education series

SELECTED TITLES IN THE SERIES

General Editor: Anthony Adams
Lecturer in Education, University of
Cambridge

DEVELOPING READERS IN THE MIDDLE YEARS

Elaine Millard

Open University Press
Buckingham • *Philadelphia*

Open University Press
Celtic Court
22 Ballmoor
Buckingham
MK18 1XW

and

1900 Frost Road, Suite 101
Bristol, PA 19007, USA

First Published 1994

A catalogue record of this book is available from the British Library

ISBN 0 335 19071 5 (pbk)

Library of Congress Cataloging-in-Publication Data

Millard, Elaine.
    Developing readers in the middle years / Elaine Millard.
       p.   cm. — (English, language, and education series)
    Includes bibliographical references (p.   ) and index.
    ISBN 0–335–19071–5
    1. Reading (Elementary)—Great Britain.   2. Curriculum planning—
Great Britain.   I. Title.   II. Series.
LB1573.M493   1994
372.41—dc20   93–29245
                                                                  CIP

Typeset by Graphicraft Typesetters Ltd, Hong Kong
Printed in Great Britain by Biddles Ltd, Guildford and King's Lynn

To my mother and father who were never too busy to read with me.

Contents

Acknowledgements

I wish to thank Marcia Puckey and all her staff at Hempshill Hall Primary School, Nottinghamshire, for their endless patience in letting me take up precious non-contact time with talk about reading and their children's responses to the joint activities we devised. In particular, I am grateful to Stuart Harrison and Pauline Davies who allowed me into their classrooms and let me share their children's work as it progressed.

General editor's introduction

Debates about reading and reading standards are always with us. But it is clear to most, probably all, teachers that the academic argument between those who argue for a phonics-based approach and those who argue that from the beginning reading must be based upon meaning, is a barren one. All teachers know that there is no single royal road to reading and that good practice in this area must be based upon a mixture of methods and, especially, that different methods will need to be used at different times with different children. In other words, in teaching reading we have above all to understand and respect the individuality of each reader.

We must focus primarily upon the reader rather than the method of teaching reading. It has been well said that there is no point in teaching a child to read unless he or she continues to do so once the skill of reading has been learned. Moreover, reading skills are not unitary, they are subtle and complex and need to be nurtured throughout a child's progress through the reading curriculum. One of the good things that a National Curriculum should ensure is more emphasis on this element of continuity in the teaching of reading, as in other respects. All too often in the past, reading has been seen to be something that ought to have been taught to children at the stage before they came into our classroom. Many secondary teachers in particular saw the teaching of reading as something that should have been completed before the child left primary school. The Bullock Report, in its excellent and eclectic account of reading, emphasizes the need for recognizing that the teaching of reading is a continuous process and not one that has an arbitrary cut-off point. Moreover, in its advocacy of 'language across the curriculum', it also stresses the importance of all teachers at every stage seeing themselves as teachers of reading. Elaine Millard, in discussing interviews with children in their first year of secondary school, records them as being 'particularly disappointing because most of the reading tasks described had narrative or poetry as the main focus and were part of the work in English lessons'. When the Bullock Report was published, I well remember a distinguished Professor of Education saying to me that none of the student teachers in his department on a PGCE course would ever have to teach reading since they were all training to be teachers in secondary schools. More recently, the National Foundation for Educational Research has conducted a survey of the role of the teaching of reading in teacher education. I was told by a mathematics colleague when we discussed our response to the survey in the department where I work, that he did not see that he needed to teach anything about reading to his mathematics students – secondary pupils who could not read were a problem for the English or special needs departments.

When attitudes such as these persist, even in 1993 among otherwise enlightened people engaged in the training of future generations of teachers, it is not surprising that, notwithstanding the excellence of much that is going on in schools, there is still a long way to go.

In this book Elaine Millard shows what we can do in practice about these issues. I welcome very much her emphasis, implicit in the title, on the idea of continuity in the reading process and, in particular, the account in Chapter 3 of the importance of building what she calls 'communities of readers', something not unrelated to Frank Smith's notion of the 'literacy club'. Her emphasis on the notion of eclecticism in reading is important also. One of the many problems in many schools and high street shops is the limited range of books that are available to parents, teachers and, therefore, to children. The Australian lecturer in English education, Ken Watson, himself a contributor to this series, was horrified a few years ago when working with me in Cambridge, to discover that in many local schools pupils were not allowed to take books home with them owing to the scarcity of provision within the funding allocated to the school. He even went so far as to write a letter to *The Times* (which was published) to lament this fact. Quite rightly he asked how we could expect to develop readers if books were not readily available to pupils to read outside as well as inside the classroom. The 'literacy club' must have doors which are always open and which are wide enough to welcome all comers, an issue Elaine Millard explores when she discusses how some groups of readers may be marginalized unless the range of what is available is sufficiently wide.

It is certainly important for children's attitudes to reading that books should not just be seen as an activity practised in school by pupils. They need to see their teachers and family read as well. The anecdotes given here of the influence of parental and sibling attitudes to reading are supported by some of the research findings of my students.

While disassociating myself entirely from those who would argue that there has been a decline in standards of reading, I would certainly agree that standards are not yet high enough – could they ever be? There is still a need for more teachers of older pupils to take reading seriously as one of their responsibilities. This applies especially to the need to do more to help pupils to become efficient readers of texts of all kinds. One of the areas that is most neglected in schools is the effective teaching of study skills and Chapter 7 of the present volume makes a valuable contribution here.

The final chapter of the book deals with the assessment of reading and, in the present climate, this is clearly of importance. The author stresses here also the importance of continuity and the need to root assessment firmly in the regular practice of the classroom. The eleven points made here grow out of the book as a whole and form a fitting conclusion to a work in which continuity has been the keynote.

It could be argued that there is a plenitude of books about the theory of the teaching of reading already available to teachers. The current volume is well grounded in the whole range of such theory but is especially strong on its application to the classroom in the middle years of schooling. There will be few teachers who will not find both help and inspiration in its pages. It contains rather more in the way of illustrations of pupils' work than is usual in this series. This emphasizes its practicality and incorporates the classroom into the book in an especially delightful way. Enjoy it.

Anthony Adams

Introduction

This book grew out of a short-term study into what children know about themselves as readers at a transition stage in their education, marked for most 11-year olds by the move from primary to secondary school. Its intention is to focus on the methods most widely used in the latter stages of primary schools to develop fluency and breadth in reading and to discuss their role in preparing pupils for the demands of the next stage of learning. Two interweaving strands of information underpin my argument. The first strand was provided by a group of 16 10- and 11-year-old pupils, interviewed on two separate occasions in a small research study on attitudes to reading in the middle years of schooling and supported by evidence from their written work. The second, more practical, strand arises out of work I developed with teachers in one of the schools in the survey who were keen to encourage their pupils' involvement with books in general, and, in particular, their knowledge about the language of story.

In the build up to the implementation of the Education Reform Act 1988, I was involved in developing strategies to help teachers decide how to assess and record reading attainment and was particularly concerned with the transition between primary and secondary practice. I set myself the task of finding out something of what children had learned about the nature of reading during the first two stages of their education. In particular I wanted to determine how well their overall experience of books and reading in the primary school had prepared them to meet the demands of the secondary school curriculum and conversely, if secondary teachers made good use of the foundations laid by their primary colleagues. Another intention was to identify examples of good practice in the primary phase which might inform the programmes of study in the secondary school and vice versa. I also wanted to determine if on the whole children at the end of their primary school phase had developed a positive view of themselves as readers and if they were being asked to behave as independent readers in the whole range of work undertaken in school.

The central message of the previous major national report on the state of the nation's language learning produced by the Bullock Committee (DES, 1975) had been that language was central to all aspects of learning and that every subject carried a responsibility for the development of reading and writing (DES, 1975: 191):

> Subject teachers need to be aware of the processes involved, able to provide the variety of reading material that is appropriate, and willing to see it as their responsibility to help their pupils meet the reading demands of their subject. The variety of written forms a child encounters will be an influence upon the development of his reading abilities. To restrict the first can result in limiting the second.

Bullock was followed by two Schools Council projects in the area of reading for information, *Extending Beginning Reading* (Southgate *et al.*, 1981) and *The Effective Use of Reading* (Lunzer and Gardner, 1979). The latter which is still the most comprehensive study of the incidence and context of classroom reading and reading set as homework in the top class of junior school and the first year of secondary, found that continuous reading tasks were usually set for homework whilst at school reading was limited to 'short bursts' of about 1–15 seconds for 50 per cent of all reading across all subjects.

As a profession, teachers have still not collected sufficient classroom-based information about how children conceptualize the process of reading after the initial stages of fluency have been established and we have only a patchy understanding of to what extent pupils make effective use of their reading competencies, either during the school day or in their leisure time. Whenever surveys of reading in school are conducted, teachers' claims that no specific period is set aside for reading because reading is everywhere embedded in the curriculum cannot be substantiated.

I particularly wanted to know if the work of these researchers had influenced practice and if almost two decades later, thoughtful reading directed to specific aims had become a central feature of all curriculum areas in the later stages of the junior school and in the first years of secondary education. My research process involved seeking different perspectives on the styles of learning developing within the classroom, by direct observation, feedback from teachers and pupils through structured interviews and finally by sampling the pupils' written work, particularly their narrative writing. The process of action research was more difficult to direct as an outside observer rather than as a classroom practitioner but it did have the advantage of allowing access to a range of classrooms for comparison of the findings and of bringing a third perspective into play.

Starting from an initial intention to find out how much pupils understood about the reading processes they used in the classroom, I aimed to get snapshots of what they would consider to be an appropriate reading task in particular contexts. I also wanted to compare the viewpoints of the teachers and pupils to discover to what extent their values matched each other. I wanted to see if what was taught and what was learned about reading in the schools I visited had a coherence and whether the experience of children at the top end of the primary school had prepared them for the demands of the next stage of their education. Children and their teachers were therefore interviewed in the final term of their primary schools. I then followed up these initial interviews with a 'story of reading' questionnaire filled in by all the interviewees' year group towards the end of the first term in their secondary school and then followed by a second round of interviews.

To help the classes write the 'story' of their reading so far, I used a set of printed guidelines which they could adapt to their own use. This was a technique their teachers welcomed as a good starting point for recording progress in that year's reading. The children's ages ranged from 10 years at the first interview to 13 years at the time of the second interview.

The interviews were loosely structured round a pre-arranged interview schedule with a kernel of set questions put to the children in a standardized form; but I varied the order according to the pupils' responses so that the answers given to the first questions determined to some extent the pattern of each particular conversation. This was to ensure that pupils were given space to elaborate initial ideas and to reflect on their particular experience of reading. Similarly the teachers' interview schedules allowed for a range of responses to be followed up and main concerns to be elaborated. The interviews were conducted where possible in informal settings and I made sure that none of the children thought they were being tested or assessed in any way and could speak freely about their own interests and opinions. The mismatch I discovered between the responses of pupils and their teachers are at the heart of this book, providing me with a basis for a discussion of what it might mean to teach reading in the middle years more effectively.

The main aim of the project on which this book is based, was to find out if attention to reading had been significantly changed since the period in the late 1970s when Whitehead *et al.* (1977) had revealed gaps in children's reading experience. The data I collected does not lend itself readily to statistical analysis nor is it the intention of this book to give a detailed picture of a whole age group. Rather I will suggest ways in which teachers might investigate classroom practice to determine how effective their own provision within the reading curriculum has been in shaping pupils' reading practices. The data I collected was used to look for significant points of agreement or disagreement between the views of the children and those expressed by their teachers. I then used the differences I uncovered as the starting point for questioning the theoretical basis underpinning teaching of reading in the middle years of schooling. I have combined these reflections with examples of classroom practice that some of the teachers I worked with developed to encourage their pupils to read with understanding, appreciation and enjoyment and which allowed their pupils to deal with more difficult and varied material both inside and outside of the school environment.

This book, therefore, is about reading communities, those that children develop for themselves and those that that teachers are building for the children in school. It stresses the way that pupils' differing experiences of the importance of reading in their lives is shaped to a greater or lesser extent by each of these communities and suggests ways in which teacher intervention can challenge readers to deepen and enrich their initial responses to books. The current emphasis on school-based or 'on-the-job' learning for teachers in training makes it essential that schools and their teachers develop strategies for researching their own classrooms and monitoring the effect of their pupils' responses. It may be argued that the National Curriculum already provides a structure for assessing and recording achievement in all aspects of the language curriculum. The problem is that these assessments identify a level of achievement on a particular occasion. They do not suggest ways of discovering what attitudes at work in the classroom will either confirm pupils as life-long readers or alienate whole classes of children.

My intention is to provide teachers with a snapshot of the status of reading in schools at a critical time. It is critical for children, because they will move from the relative security of a classroom, with a single teacher who knows their strengths and weaknesses in detail, to a much larger institution where many more demands will be placed on their ability to adapt to variety of complex curriculum contexts and where reading will become a major vehicle of their individual learning. It is also a critical time for teachers, because the introduction of the National Curriculum has created new demands for teachers to establish criteria for assessing the effectiveness of their reading provision and to collect evidence of how far these criteria are being met. Teachers need to be asking the sort of questions that will give them a broader view of how their practice contributes to pupils' perceptions of what it is to be a proficient and active reader in the context of both school and society as a whole.

For the past decade the emphasis on reading development has been on a personal engagement between reader and text that has worked to minimize the responsibilities of the teachers in developing their pupils' knowledge of the shared conventions and reading strategies that bring the written page into being. This has had the effect of placing an emphasis on the pleasure element in reading, associated with narratives that embody worlds that are already familiar to young readers. This is often at the expense of widening and deepening the young reader's choice and understanding of more demanding and less familiar ways of telling.

The first part of this book is concerned with the processes of learning to read and discusses the messages that particular methods of instruction may give both teachers and learners about what it is to be a good reader. Some of the consequences of concentrating on individual preference and performance in reading in the middle years are identified, with the intention of helping teachers audit their own curriculum provision for reading and identifying gaps or areas for future development.

In the second part of the book, the focus is on more practical ways a group of teachers developed for literature-based work with primary school children and also addresses ways of improving reading for information and sharing understandings with each other. There are also suggestions for meeting the National Curriculum's emphasis on developing a more explicit knowledge about the organization and structure of both narrative and non-fiction texts. The final chapter suggests ways in which teachers and their pupils can keep more detailed records of reading attainment and discusses ways in which more continuous teacher assessment can be used to promote the development of reading.

PART ONE

Reading as a social contract

1 Learning to read and its legacy

'I was two years old and my dad bought me a book for my birthday on the 29th of December and it was called *Tom Kitten's Great Adventures*. I didn't know what it was first of all, then my dad read me this book and I started saying the words with him. It was really hard to read, but I soon got the hang of it. I really wanted this book because my dad always liked reading it to me. When I went to school everyone used to laugh at me because I couldn't read very well at first. It got worse later because then everyone hated me because I was a brilliant reader.'

Girl, age 11

In this statement, one of the children I interviewed, summarizes the contradictions inherent in the reading process for learners in the context of the school. First, she highlights the discontinuity between her experience of reading at home compared with what was expected by her school, and all the subsequent doubts and uncertainties about success that ensued. Second, she draws attention to the importance of peer group attitudes that helped to reinforce her insecurities. Descriptions of such experiences and their attendant anxieties reoccur quite frequently in children's accounts of learning to read.

In the stories of reading which I collected from a sample of 100 children in the first year at three contrasting comprehensive schools, a significant number described learning to read as hard. More significantly, the numbers of boys who claimed learning to read was difficult was exactly twice that of the girls. Of the 56 boys, 26, almost half the sample, described learning to read as hard, 15 thought it was easy and 15 thought it was 'all right'. A significant number of the boys qualified their accounts of reading in school with words like 'boring' or 'rubbish'.

Of the 44 girls in the sample, only 12 thought learning to read was hard, 21 thought it was easy and 11 thought it was all right. My own small survey exactly mirrors the findings of the Assessment of Performance Unit (APU, 1988) which reported a significant disparity in attitudes to reading between the sexes:

In successive interviews it has become apparent that a substantial proportion of children in school develop negative associations with the processes of reading and writing, the latter in particular. In all six surveys that have been carried out at primary level, for example, over 10 per cent of the children have indicated that they 'hate writing' and that they write as little as possible; nearly twice as many boys as girls tend to respond in this manner.

It was also reported that many children find writing about their reading onerous and so testing them in writing, about the books they have read may not be a very reliable method of assessing ability:

They also enjoyed talking, if not writing, about books they had read; but activities involving written language were generally more popular among girls than among boys.

Because early reading experiences shape pupils' subsequent attitudes to how they will approach reading in later years, it is particularly important for teachers involved in the second and third stages of learning to form a clear picture of the various strands of curriculum development that have contributed to their attitude. More importantly, the attitudes to reading that the teachers and children bring with them into the classroom will certainly influence the way a class accommodates to a reading task and create expectations for their future learning. Much of the teaching of reading has been predicated on the notion that the reading of fiction is an activity that is pleasurable in itself and the rewards of joining the literacy club are self evident to children (Smith, 1984). That this view has not been convincingly conveyed to a large number of pupils, makes it important that teachers think through their approaches to teaching reading and the kinds of pleasure they are offering.

How children learn to read

There is an antithesis governing discussions about all aspects of reading in professional journals and, more significantly, in the popular press, which sets, at one polarity, a series of hierarchically structured language skills, directed to functional purposes that can be practised through repetitive tasks and finally 'mastered', and at the other a model of 'growth' through the imaginative familiarity with stories, songs and traditional rhymes, where development is seen as continuous process. Most of the debates conducted in the national press about the teaching of reading have supported what looks like a common sense notion that reading is an elementary mechanical skill, which can be taught to all children systematically. Repeatedly in press reports about standards in reading and writing, the word 'basic' is used to suggest that all children begin from a common starting point of 'sounding out' in response to print, to build a sight vocabulary before making sense of a whole story. An example of the way the populist view of the nature of reading enforces a simple division of the learning task into decoding and then everything else is provided by a report in the *Daily Mail*, which during 1991/2 ran a series of articles strongly critical of what it saw as 'trendy' ways of teaching reading. When the results of the first Standard Assessment Tasks in reading for seven-year olds were published, the front page of the paper (15 December 1991) greeted its readers with the banner headline 'Shameful' qualified by its sub-heading 'Seven Year Olds Failed by the System'. The accompanying article was an indictment of teachers' reported ability to teach reading effectively, although the first run of these national tests had in fact shown that three-quarters of the children tested had reached a satisfactory or higher standard in the reading targets. It seemed to be being argued at the silliest extreme of what had become a very heated debate that children were failing to learn to read because their teachers had been over-concerned with introducing them to interesting books. Contrary to this popular prejudice about lack of early reading instruction most of the children in my survey showed that they had internalized the idea of reading as decoding the words. In recounting how they learned to read, over half the sample described activities such as the following:

> 'I learned to read at home and at school. The first book I brought home from school was called *Look*, on every page it just said, "look!". I also read books called Peter and Jane and Janet and John. My mum taught me to read words off some cards. When I was little I didn't like reading because I wanted my mum to read to me instead.'
>
> Girl, age 12

> 'My mum taught me to read by bringing words home, so I sounded the words out and then built them up into sentences with a lot of help. My first books were *Read It Yourself*, Ladybird Books and nursery rhymes.'
>
> Girl, age 11

> 'Mum and my teachers taught me to read. I found it hard and I soon got bored. I had stepping stones which I stepped on and I said the word that was written on the stones.'
>
> Boy, age 11

> 'I first learned to read at school. I just started reading at five. My first teacher did little words like "and or me" on cards. In my second year we did harder words and started on books with a few pages. My first books were about Roger Red Hat and Johnny and Jennifer Yellow Hat.'
>
> 'When I was in the juniors I went onto another kind of book starting with Stage One and then two years later I was on Stage Six. Then I went back to reading story books like my favourite *Charlie and the Chocolate Factory*.'
>
> Boy, age 12

These children have all been taught to read with schemes that depend on a build up of regular word patterns and for many their learning has been rein-forced with practice at recognizing individual words. The last comment sug-gests that the boy saw reading instruction as separate from the real business of reading, a kind of hiatus in his engagement with stories. Accounts which described learning with a whole-book method where books were a source of pleasure in themselves, were very much in the minority:

> 'My parents taught me to read when I was two and a half. When I was three I could read perfectly. I can remember some of my very first books. They were: *Counting to Ten*, *The Little Big Book*, and *The Sweet Millet Porridge*.
>
> Girl, age 11

One boy's account stressed the importance of the print in his environment as well as engagement with story:

> 'When I started to read, my mum and my teacher really helped a lot so I could read books and the signs in the street. At my last school we had different kinds of reading levels but I quickly passed all the levels so I could read anything in the class. The books I liked in school were adventures. I didn't like the soppy books, the kind teachers read to me about children.'
>
> Boy, age 11

> 'Mainly, I suppose my mother and father taught me. We played games with picture cards, read books together and listened to story tapes. Fortunately I loved reading and found it very easy. Of course like everybody I made slip-ups and I used to get very frustrated if I couldn't read a certain word. If I came across a new word I had to know what it meant! I had a lot of books when I was younger. Some of my favourites were: *The Tiger Who Came to Tea*, *The Very Hungry Caterpillar* and *Phoebe and the Hot Water Bottle*. I liked to read books from the school library.'
>
> Girl, age 11

This was the only account that I found in the pupils' stories of reading that could be said to describe a process of learning to read with 'real books' and even here, the method had been developed at home rather than at school.

Because linguists have been able to describe the underlying patterns that govern language production and break utterances down into their constituent parts, some 'reading specialists' have advocated that learning to read can be similarly systematized. They argue that children should be taught to 'build' texts from the smallest units of language and to sound out the phonic elements while acquiring a sight vocabulary. Other specialists have stressed that the written language is structured by more complex rules that determine the patterns that are appropriate for a wide variety of instrumental and expressive purposes. Each written format, whether it be a gas bill, a letter of application for a particular job or an experimental novel, is governed by a set of conventions that determines the appropriateness of register, vocabulary, syntax, length and printed format. A printed text can never be speech written down, even when writers aspire to the supposed 'primacy' of the spoken word and attempt its representation, as in the first section of James Joyce's *Portrait of an Artist as a Young Man* or the poems of e. e. cummings, both of which employ a great deal of artifice to create an illusion of immediacy. This viewpoint leads to the suggestion that children need to understand the purpose of the print they

encounter and the different functions it serves in the context of their lives to
make learning relevant. Recent research into early learning has stressed the
emergence of literacy and the role of parents who act as powerful role models
in sharing print activities such as writing letters and cards, sharing their
newspapers, looking for labels while shopping (Hall, 1987; Hannon, 1990;
Weinberger, Hannon and Nutbrown, 1990).

The former approach has been labelled 'bottom-up' and the whole book
approach as 'top-down' (Pumfrey, 1991: 114–23). Pumfrey argues that an ex-
clusive adherence to any one methodology has disadvantages for all learners
but particularly affects children with reading difficulties:

> The 'bottom-up' model underestimates the important effects of higher levels of
> linguistic processing, of the meaning of the text and the total experiences of the
> reader on the lower level de-coding process. The 'top-down' approach can lead
> to the sacrifice of accuracy and to failure in reconstructing the writer's message.

Pumfrey suggests that good teaching requires a combination of both approaches and this is exactly what the HMI survey (DES, 1991), undertaken in
Autumn 1990 and reported in 1991, found in schools. My own survey, however, which covered a range of primary schools feeding comprehensive schools
in three very different areas, lending some supporting evidence for the view
that schools are eclectic in their early methods of teaching reading, further
suggests that children internalize the former rather than the latter process as
what is expected of readers. Their accounts most frequently stressed 'learning
the words' and 'sounding out' as ways into reading. Further, the majority of
the books they remembered as early readers were from conventional reading
schemes where meaning is almost an irrelevancy. Moreover, as with the girl
quoted at the beginning of the chapter, reading at home and reading at school
were frequently seen as different processes.

Learning to read has legacies in the expectations it sets up of what books can
offer and how meaning is conveyed. I think it is vital that teachers of older
children have a full grasp of the issues underlying the reading debate and know
about the most common methods used to instruct young readers so that they
can trace their influence on the attitudes to reading that exist in their own
classrooms and work to build on them or to remedy failures. Phonic instruction has become central in the current debates about reading instruction and
has been given undue prominence in the rewrite of the early stages of the
National Curriculum (April 1993). Rather than using the word as a mantra to
conjure up notions of rigour and disciplined learning, it is important to go to
the reading materials associated with the method and see what else they teach.

Phonics and reading schemes

There are two main ways in which phonic awareness can be taught to children.
The first uses structured reading schemes that aim to introduce the young

reader to a set of phoneme/grapheme relationships at a time. They regularize the language by restricting vocabulary, wherever possible, to words that obey simple rules in order to establish sound–symbol relationships. An example of this is an emphasis on word 'families' that share a phonic element (e.g. rain and train, house and mouse, fox and box). They are often supplemented by work books or sheets that ask children to fill gaps in words with particular sounds matched to picture cues. The thirteenth phonic reader in the Longman *Bangers and Mash*, *The Hole Story* series provides the reader with practice recognising the 'oa' vowel diagraph. The story describes how Mum cuts up a loaf to make toast. Hot toast goes down well on a cold day. Later in the story a goat makes an appearance eating soap! In 'Things to do', the reader is asked to:

Add 'oa' and make up words from the story:
b − − t   c − − l   c − − t   g − − t
r − − d   fl − − t   gr − − ns   thr − − t

The need to work with a limited number of sounds and patterns can make the reading books appear very laboured, particularly in the first stages, as in the following example taken from an introductory reader I found in use in schools (Boyce, 1977).

The Red Lorry
Deb the rat and Meg the hen
sat in the red lorry.
Ben the dog and Jip the cat
sat in the red lorry.
Sam the fox and the fat pig
sat on the red lorry.
The lorry went up the hill
Bang
Ben and Jip fell down
Deb and Meg fell down
Sam and the fat pig
fell down.

If an adult were to tell this story to a child it might go something like this: 'One day a rat, a hen, a pig, a cat, a dog and a fox all tried to ride up a hill in a red lorry. They made the lorry so heavy that when it got half way up it broke down with a big bang and all the animals came tumbling down the hill.'

The names given to all the animals in the text serve little purpose except to give additional practice with confusing consonant sounds and introduce their capital forms. It would be more meaningful if the causal link between the overloading of the lorry and and its subsequent breakdown could be established through sentence subordination, but this is considered too difficult for the learner and all sentence links are kept implicit. *The Hole Story* does make some attempt at a logical chronological narrative, however tenuous the links, something that is more difficult to find in the following phonic reader, particularly aimed at children with early reading difficulties:

this is a black box
buzz buzz buzz
goes the black box
buzz buzz buzz
stop the buzz
stop stop the buzz
an egg is under the box
buzz buzz goes the egg
crack goes the egg
crack crack crack
up jumps a fuzzbuzz
this is the fuzzbuzz
buzz goes the fuzzbuzz
buzz buzz buzz
the fuzzbuzz jumps
the fuzzbuzz jumps up
up and up and up
jumps the fuzzbuzz
and the fuzzbuzz
goes under the egg

Much more sophisticated reading between the lines is required to understand that the narrative announces the hatching out of the fuzzbuzz, a creature which will feature in all the following books in the scheme. Not only is the storyline difficult to follow, but the text is completely lacking in punctuation, so that only line breaks give an idea of the sentences, all of which seem oddly short and incomplete. At one point a voice intrudes, 'stop the buzz, stop stop the buzz', with no indication of who or what is speaking and who is being addressed. It has a surreal quality added to by the fact that the text is also peppered with other commands for the reader to obey such as:

write: the black box goes buzz

or

draw and colour the egg

Whatever purpose there is for reading the words, or completing the suggested activities, it remains an instructor's purpose rather than a narrative purpose. The sounds of particular letters are being reinforced by repeated practice. What a child can make of the story or understand about the process of reading from such exercises it is hard to imagine, except perhaps the concept of 'learning the words'. In some phonic readers, however, the ingenuity of the author in using the sound correspondences leads to anarchic nonsense rhymes, which children find both enjoyable and memorable as in the beginner series of the *Dr Seuss* readers, where the repetition of key sounds, is reinforced by rhythm and rhymes so that the language is memorable and fun to read out loud.

Patterning is also feature of many folk tales and nursery rhymes and is also used to good effect by writers in young children's picture books such as Eve Sutton's *My Cat Likes to Hide in Boxes* and Quentin Blake's *Mr Magnolia*. The predictability of the rhyme in these stories, reinforced by the rhythm of the prose helps to make the words memorable and provides a support for anticipating meaning.

Teachers who use a story-book method use these particular stories and others like them to help the learning of language patterns, avoiding the more forced repetitions of the scheme books. The message phonic readers give to the learner is that reading is repetitive practice of sounds and words, something to learn before you go onto books that make sense. Some children never see the point. Not all early readers use phonic correspondence as their main feature but repetition of vocabulary is a central feature of all reading schemes and a particular feature of the keywords approach to early readers. The books employ a carefully controlled sight vocabulary in simple sentences to encourage the memorization of the most commonly recurring words in the English language. The initial research on which the keywords research was based was conducted by McNally and Murray (1968) and was based on the frequency of vocabulary found in adult and children's reading matter. The method is also sometimes called 'Look and Say' and the reading scheme books are usually supplemented with flash cards which test children's recognition of the words they are learning. The Ladybird reading scheme with its stories of Peter and Jane and their red setter dog, Pat, is the best known example of this reading method. The sentence structure is kept simple, beginning with imperatives, 'Look, Jane, Look' and progressing to sentences made up of a subject and verb, 'I can jump,' and then a subject, verb, object, 'Jane likes the dog, the dog likes Jane.' The stories revolve around the daily events assumed to be part of the experience of every child, but which mainly reflect the habits of a white, middle-class, nuclear family. Critics of these reading schemes such have demonstrated the emptiness of their meaning by reading the texts from back to front to illustrate their lack of chronology or narrative logic (Wade, 1990: 21–3). The individual books in the series have been written not to entertain their readers or to give interesting information but to ensure sufficient repetition of particular words and sentence forms. Prior experience of story form will not help predict the next sentence in the sequence as it will, for example, in any telling of *The Three Little Pigs* because reading schemes are rarely based on narrative logic.

Newer reading schemes are a little more imaginative in content but no less stilted in their syntactic structure. Whereas *Dr Zeuss* books and traditional nursery rhymes employ repetition alongside rhythm and rhyme to make reading both predictable and memorable, the latter may use repetition alone. The following example is from the popular new scheme *The Oxford Reading Tree* (1986) and is classified as a Stage Four, Book Three reader. It is called *Come In!* a title that carries little sense of a story waiting to be told. Here it is in its entirety:

Dad was painting the door.
Mum went out.
Wilf and Wilma came to play.
'Come in,' said Dad.
Three children came to the house.
They came to play with Biff.
'Come in,' said Biff.
Four children came to the house.
They came to play with Chip.
'Come in,' said Chip.
Five children came to the house.
They wanted to play with Kipper.
'Come in,' said Kipper.
Mum came home.
'What a lot of children
What a lot of mess.'
Mum looked for Biff, Chip and Kipper.
They were watching television.
Mum was cross.
Mum gave the children some biscuits.
They all went home.
Mum went outside.
'Oh no,' said Mum.

                                                            Roderick Hunt

The story has an obvious instructional purpose. It is, however, not the kind of narrative purpose that a familiarity with imaginative stories would lead a reader to expect, but a piece of language instruction to establish the different use of the present and past tenses, 'come' and 'came'. Each utterance is presented separately and the narrative logic of the incidents is kept implicit. The reader has to make use of the supporting illustrations, which are colourful and humorous, to understand the connections. The work of establishing the story's context and characters is also left to the pictures. In fact, the story's ending on mum's exasperated, 'Oh no!,' makes no sense at all without the final picture which shows Mum looking out at a group of dogs who also expect a biscuit.

The pattern of writing in the whole scheme adheres to the principle of a build up of language through a gradual introduction of vocabulary and verb forms with minimal textual cohesive ties of syntax, through conjunction and subordination. There is little inversion and few examples of the use of passive constructions, even in the most advanced of the texts. By Stage Seven, Book Seven, *The Red Planet* (1987) still uses the simplest of sentence constructions and omits subordinating conjunctions:

Wilf came to play with Chip.
They made a rocket out of bits and pieces.
The rocket looked quite good.

Wilf and Chip played in the rocket ship.
They pretended to be spacemen.

                                                                    Roderick Hunt

In their writing, however, children are expected to develop ideas using the characteristics of different genres and having a sense of both purpose and audience. Katherine Perera (1993) has also pointed to the way some stories in early reading schemes simply stop without creating any sense of completion and how they muddle tenses when a narrator introduces a direct address to a particular character. She also shows how lack of variation in sentence length and structure coupled with the avoidance of pronouns leads to language that is stilted and unnatural sounding. If reading and writing are more closely connected than speech and written forms, then reading schemes offer a very limited model.

Books for the early stages of reading frequently imply a 'textually bound' reader who is not expected to use outside cues other than the pictures. Reading is presented as a matter of de-coding what is in the text by moving from part to whole, stumbling to sound out unfamiliar words and learning a sight vocabulary through constant repetition and practice. Stories are irrelevant and meaning secondary to sound–sight relationships. The reading scheme 'method' particularly appeals to non-specialists, because it appears to deliver a rigorous structure and disciplined learning process, although for the main it depends on exactly the same process of retaining a sight vocabulary as other kinds of reading require. The assumption is that developing readers read specifically to learn about reading, rather than for pleasure or information. Individual words, their formation and the rate of introduction of new vocabulary take precedence over narrative complexity. The children in the survey call this 'learning the words' and it has formed a part of most of their learning process. It leads to a different set of values being used to select appropriate reading for the younger age group than the ones used in choosing books for older readers because the beginner reader's interest in what is being read is a secondary concern to that of level of ability. The early readers hope to ease the new reader along by the repetition of words and simple phrases. The older schemes print list of words at the end of each 'book' to test this recognition and recall. Both phonic and 'Look and Say' reading schemes bear little relationship to the kinds of books children would choose to read for themselves and though many generations of children have succeeded in working their way through colours and levels to become readers, it is not such stories that help them to develop a knowledge of how stories are structured or increase their understanding of the world. At best they are a means to an end; at worst, they hinder children's understanding that reading has a purpose. A late reader child on such books for a long period of time is likely to develop what Barry Wade (1990) has vividly described as 'reading rickets'.

The critic of children's fiction, Margery Fisher (1970: 17), describes choosing such a book with her eldest granddaughter, a late reader of nearly eight:

'I was thinking in theoretical terms. I thought, "Ah, yes reluctant reader, repetition to help her along. And I found an easy book with a repetitive pattern. When she came to the fourth repetition of words and situations she heaved a great sigh and said, "Not again." So I left her by the bookshelf.'

Whole-language approaches

In counteracting a mechanistic, programmed view of the learning process, other theorists have stressed the natural development of language skills in children, positing a growth model for the written form of the language based on the model of spoken language acquisition (Clay, 1979; Wells, 1985). Their work has demonstrated the importance of children being introduced at an early age to the conventions of print if they are to become confident readers in school. Gordon Wells' longitudinal study of 120 children in Bristol concluded that the most important factor in the development of young children's language skills was an early experience of story and an essential element of this was interaction with an adult who was able to mediate the text to the child. Interaction with adults in storying activities introduced children to what Wells calls 'disembedded language' familiarizing them with more abstract and de-contextualized structures, particularly formal syntactical ones. He concluded that a literate family background, where reading and writing occurred daily were the best indicators of success in the early stages of schooling. Children need adult guidance in learning how print works and to gain familiarity with a range of genres and purposes for writing.

A range of classroom practices, best described as a 'Language Experience' approach, have evolved from the observations of how very young children learn to recognise words and letter shapes prior to formal instruction. Many children, particularly those from families where books and literacy are highly valued, come to school with clear ideas of what reading and writing activities entail. Every teacher of reading, who is also a parent, remembers with pleasure the first time their child recognises print in the environment. My own son pointed to the cover of a book on a rack I was flicking round to choose a new picture book to share with him and said, 'That says Jonathan, there.' He was three years old and the book was called *Jonathan Just*. I wasn't surprised he could 'read' the word because all his books were clearly labelled with his name as were his coat peg, slipper bag and the anorak he wore to nursery class. The book's title used the plain sans serif print familiar in his classroom. The shop assistant was amazed that so small a child could read but of course he was not reading as such, but displaying 'readerly behaviour' in recognising a familiar word that had personal significance. My second son at a similar age could recognise the French word 'jouet' on the windows and sign boards of Brittany shops because he was so determined to track down the small Majorette cars that were his passion once such shops had been pointed out to him on several previous occasions.

Many children, in a similar way, recognize the McDonald signs and logos or ice-cream names, because these products play a major part in their lives. Margaret Meek (1990: 145–54) puts it like this: 'to be born into a literate society is to encounter language in print in the world at large before learning to read in school'. In order to build on what is seen as a natural process of language acquisition, the infant teacher uses both the child's individual experience and opportunities shared in class to create meaningful contexts for reading and writing. The emphasis is on using language for real purposes in real situations rather than learning in a de-contextualized way. Children are encouraged to record their responses often in a drawing and the teacher scribes the child's own words as a caption, sentence or small story. *Break Through to Literacy* materials which were designed by a Schools Council Project to facilitate language experience approaches are part of the process. They consist of a plastic stand or 'sentence maker', and a folder which held word cards with commonly used words with spaces to add the child's increasing sight vocabulary. Children compose their own stories to share with their teachers and classmates using these sentence makers. The language has therefore been provided by the child and so it is much more predictable when read back helping the child to gain confidence. The approach has the added advantage of confirming the interconnectedness of writing and reading. Some teachers extend the practice by allowing children to create a dialogue with them by writing a response at the bottom of each new piece of writing, often in the form question to which the child can add a written response. The teacher uses her questions both as a way of testing the learner's understanding and to encourage further writing.

Language development can be further encouraged through structured learning situations such as creative play. Schools build on the 'natural' impulse to make sense of print in the environment by creating learning situations in which the need to use print to record information and read it back to others is part of the play process. A corner of the classroom becomes a garden centre, a newsagents or a veterinary surgery and purposeful role play enables learners to expand their linguistic horizons. In such situations reading and writing are given a purpose and a meaning through inviting the learner into membership of a literate community. In Frank Smith's (1984: 1) description, as an apprentice:

> Children learn to use and to understand spoken language by being admitted into the club of spoken language users. Experienced members of the club accept children as apprentices who are expected to become practitioners in due course. The seniors demonstrate all the advantages of the club to the newcomers and collaborate in helping them to participate in all the activities. Children become literate by joining a similar club on similar terms.

In describing this process as 'growth' it is easy to mask the importance of the supporting social context that makes it possible for small children to identify literate behaviour and wish to mimic it. Shirley Brice Heath's ethnographic study has detailed the 'different social legacies' in two Carolinan rural communities that shape children's attitudes to literacy and consequently their attitude to the tasks of reading and writing in school. She argued that the different ways children learned to use language depended on 'the ways in which each community structured their families, defined the roles that community members could assume, and played out their concepts of childhood that guided child socialisation' (Heath, 1983: 11). One of the communities she studied was black, the other white, but it was not a racial difference or, as is frequently assumed, a difference between oral and literate traditions, that determined their attitudes. One of the findings for the children of the black community was their inexperience in 'labelling' activities and their lack of pre-school experience of identifying the discrete elements of a particular object or scene made them unable to give appropriate answers to questions where they were asked to distinguish one thing from another. The children of the white community, on the other hand, had no experience of developing extended imaginative narratives. Simply stated, school work, particularly methods of teaching reading and writing depended on attitudes to the printed word which were positioned outside the experience of both the communities, but which matched the aspirations of the townspeople, who were used as a control group.

Margaret Clark's study of young fluent British readers through interviews with their parents also showed that those children who made excellent progress in reading at school had had a wide and varied diet of reading materials at home which ranged from *The Financial Times* advice columns to comics, train timetables, cookery books and encyclopedias (Clark, 1976).

> That the attributes of the particular child were an important aspect of the situation is not denied but the crucial role of the environment, the experiences which the child obtained, their relevance to his interest and the willingness of the adults to encourage and to build upon these, should not be underestimated.

Clark's findings about the wide range of reading material that, in a supportive context, young children choose to read, have implications for schools in ensuring that children with potential, but without the continuing support of the kind available to most of the children whom she interviewed, have access to material to suit their developing interests and to motivate their reading. Language experience approaches need to introduce children to new print media as well as using their prior knowledge. Successful teaching involves children in a wide range of experiences, including printed materials, which encourage the further development of both spoken and written language. Less successful teaching limits children to their existing knowledge and means of expression, and does not introduce them to more formal, or structured, written forms of the language that are essential for success in school. The language they practise in reading their own written transcripts is more closely related to the spoken than the written word and does not expand understanding or create an interest in words for themselves.

The story approach

The next major contribution to theories about the early learning of reading is found in the ways in which teachers work to engage their children's interest in book language so that they begin to understand the conventions of story telling and can use their knowledge of its vocabularies and syntactical structures to predict meaning when reading a new text. Just as there is a strong cultural component to the development understanding of the role print plays in the community and its uses as a medium of communication, so culture plays a large part in the kinds of stories children encounter and the ways in which these are presented to them.

Barbara Hardy's (1975) suggestion that the making and telling of stories is a primary act of mind and as such, the birth right of every human being, has been widely quoted to justify the teaching of literature. Indeed, every culture, each community, shares ways of telling their own experience and the exploits of their predecessors to each other. Children's earliest independent writing takes the form of a chronologically structured recounts of what they have experienced. Stories and the way they are told, however, do not flow of necessity into a single universally understood format, but depend heavily on learned patterns of making meaning. The French structuralist enterprise described by Roland Barthes (1974) as an attempt to discover a blueprint for 'all the world's stories (and there have been ever so many) within a single structure' exploded into the more individualistic methodology of *S/Z* whose system of codes, devised to unlock the underlying patterns of meaning in a story, taps into culturally determined ways of establishing character, suspense and actions, which Barthes terms 'blocks of signification'. Barthes demonstrates how the meaning of a given text is called into being by the reader's prior knowledge gleaned from other texts and other stories met in the past. The implications of this for teaching are, that if children are to develop as readers with an interest in story and the creative use of language, then the teaching of reading needs to be in the context of meaningful prose and engaging narrative.

It is because of the universal appeal of the story form (a pull so seductive that Plato was reluctant to allow it a place in the education of his guardians), and its power to instruct through pleasure, that the teaching of reading is largely conducted through the medium of narrative fiction (even when this takes on a form as 'empty' as some of the 'stories' written for reading schemes) and we expect children to develop an understanding of the structure of narrative in the early stages of learning to read. Margaret Meek, whose work is founded on her strong conviction that 'beginner readers' should be enabled to 'discover the power and the excitement of reading, not simply its usefulness as a skill for information retrieval', has frequently demonstrated the lessons that children learn from imaginative fiction, particularly their early picture books. These, she argues, in the interweaving of picture and text, provide a rich resource for exploring experience while at the same time introducing the young reader to ambiguity, irony and symbolic language. The individual voices of the writers and the variety of linguistic devices employed give children varied experience of story form and models of ways of shaping stories (Meek, 1988).

Children who have access from an early age to good picture stories learn that reading is pleasurable and are encouraged to be self-motivated in their reading, adding to their understanding of how stories are structured. This means that the books we choose for reading with children need to challenge rather than confirm their understanding of the way print works and ideas are presented.

When they are reading to children there is a tendency for adults to choose simplified texts with bland sentence structures that do not ask the learner to work at understanding. When adults write about their own experiences of learning to read, however, it is often a 'difficult' text that they claim captured their attention and imagination and provoked the curiosity necessary for learning. The method of teaching reading grounded in these insights has been termed 'the story approach' and draws on the power of story to engage the full interest of its reader, thereby supplying cues of meaning. The method rests on the research of psycho-linguists like Kenneth Goodman (1982) who described the implicit knowledge a reader needs to bring to the text in order to predict both its structure and meanings on the basis of selected cues. The emphasis is on de-coding to meaning rather than de-coding to sound in a process where the reader is engaged actively with the author through the printed page.

There are two main strands found in the practice of most teachers. The most common of these is an individualized reading approach based on an individual grading collections or schemes of stories arranged loosely into levels of difficulty (for example, see Moon, 1980). The key to success of the method depends on the matching of children and books so teachers need to be skilled in assessing the levels of the books they use and give enough time for individualized conferences to guide children in their choice. The collections suggested are eclectic and include some units of reading schemes as well as good children's fiction.

The variation of a story book approach that has been given most popular attention however is the method described as 'Reading with Real Books'. Here the teacher is far more pro-active in introducing children to good writing in the form of story and picture books. Stories are an essential part of the classroom experience and language work is built around themes arising out of the stories. The power of imaginative writing to draw a child into learning is illustrated by Helen Savva's analysis of Maurice Sendak's *Where the Wild Things Are* (Taylor, 1991):

> Young children encountering the book for the first time are likely to identify with a small boy whose wolf suit looks like a 'baby-grow' (which has ears and claws) and who is about to land himself in great trouble . . . In the very first illustration we see that Max has constructed a den. He ties handkerchiefs

together to make a line and hammers this into the wall causing it to crack. He stands on books! And he hangs his teddy up by the arm. The opening sentence of the text which accompanies the illustration leaves us hanging in mid air:

'The night Max wore his wolf suit and made mischief of one kind . . .' and we must turn the page to read:

'and another'.

This line of text is accompanied by a picture which shows Max chasing a terrier around with a fork – what might Max do with a fork if he ever catches the dog? Again the text leaves us in suspense and we must turn the page. We are caught up in the narrative. The text and the illustrations together propel us into the story.

Accounts of work with children based on a real book approach have been written by Jill Bennett (1982), Liz Waterland (1985) and Hilary Minns (1989). When the real book method is properly implemented it demands frequent interaction between the child and the adult who is modelling the reading process. Children need both time to read and someone to listen. Many schools therefore engage the co-operation of parents and stress the importance of children being able to read to someone at home. This is often called 'Paired Reading' or described as a 'Partnership Scheme' and was at the heart of Barbara Bush's message to parents when, as a member of the American Literacy Program, she urged American parents, 'To read to your kids, hug 'em and read to them.'

A similar emphasis on child and adult interacting through a shared experience of a text is at the heart of the 'Shared Reading' method which has been described most fully by Don Holdaway (1979). The focus is on large books (Big Books) with big print used with all the class for reading-aloud sessions. Sharing helps children who are not confident to participate in the reading. Teachers encourage children to see particular aspects of the text as they read, letter–sound relationships for example, building up phonemic awareness. Teachers write the books with their classes as well as using enlarged versions of popular published stories which children can share together and then meet as individual readers. Children gain confidence through familiarity with the language of the stories. Holdaway emphasises the importance of a core of texts which are revisited regularly and because they are well known through shared reading can then support individuals in their early independent reading.

Story books have valuable language lessons to teach children about the structure and organization of the written forms of the language. Mike Taylor (1991: 58–64) has further described the richness of the language features of early picture books, detailing specific ways in which these texts help children develop knowledge about language. These include chaining of items in lists, repeated syntactic frames, the use of direct speech, conscious play with tense forms and the repetition of phonemic patterns through alliteration, rhyme and word play.

A further word about phonics

Like 'Standard English' and 'Shakespeare', the label 'phonics' has been used in the present debate about reading as an indicator of traditional, and by implication, successful ways of teaching. It has been used to flag a particular view of reading, which is really advocating a return to the use of graded reading schemes to introduce regular patterns of sound/print representation in a formal way. As I pointed out above, phonemic awareness is readily developed without de-contextualized drills and all teachers use phonic instruction of some kind. However, the suggestion of many politicians and right-wing advisers has been that teachers have wilfully ignored the role of phonic understanding in their reading programmes and consequently children are not developing effective reading strategies.

The central idea of a programmed approach to phonics is that children can develop reading skills incrementally, working from simple relationships of consonant and vowels sounds in common words, to more complex blends of both. These are introduced in such a way as to demonstrate the regularity of the system and to teach rules such as the American favourite, 'when two vowels go walking the first one does the talking'.

An ability to work out how to recognize words that are new is an important one and one that no teacher of early readers would wish to ignore. Recognition of letter–sound relationships form part of nearly every early-years teacher's repertoire. For example, when children encounter one word that blends 'ch' into a single sound they will be encouraged to think of other words that share this sound–symbol relationship such as 'chair, church, chicken, cherry, chose' and perhaps on a separate occasion have their attention drawn to examples where the sound is not blended in as in the word 'school'. Indeed, research evidence shows that sounding out is the one strategy that failing readers readily fall back on with unfamiliar words, with mixed success. What teachers who value the power of the stories they share with children question is the need to teach these skills divorced from the reality of engaging with meaning in a purposeful way. They prefer to integrate these skills within the context of other purposeful reading activities.

Developing phonemic awareness

In working with stories and poetry, teachers therefore frequently choose books which make use of repetition, rhyme and structure within a meaningful context, and they draw their pupils' attention to the word patterns and the shape of the written form of the language they encounter, while they read and write. This is frequently achieved in the writing of shared stories where the teacher transcribes the ideas created by the class. As she writes, the teacher models the process of transcription, drawing her classes' attention to the way words are written and the shape they make on the page, looking particularly at beginnings and endings of words and regular blends of consonants and vowels. What is being taught is phonemic awareness, that is the knowledge that sounds are presented by certain combinations of letters. The work will be further reinforced when handwriting is practised using particular combinatons of letters and may be further supported by word games. When children are writing independently they will be helped to spell the new words in their compositions by reference to words they already know and which have particular visual patterns. Good habits of spelling are encouraged by helping the child to form a visual image of the new word rather than through spelling out. Children are asked to use a look–cover–write–check routine whenever a new word is requested. First the learner looks carefully at the word while the teacher points out features that will help to fix in the memory what is seen, such as its phonic family or a word within a word. The word is then covered and the learner has to write the word from memory before checking to see if the word is correct. The memorizing is vital because copying a word alone does not help children memorize spellings.

What is important to note is that all the research into early learning that I have reviewed stresses the important role played by children's early experience of print in shaping their future attitudes to reading. Positive experiences and achievement of both pleasure in story and teacher approval through progress, predispose children to read for themselves and to choose appropriately if a wide selection of reading is made available to them. A history of failure, however, developed by the slow struggle to make half sense of meaningless text predisposes the learner to avoid the reading task altogether and find alternative routes to self-esteem and success, sometimes in the form of disruptive and challenging behaviour. The story of the Yorkshire child who, when asked why he was reading a particular book by one of Her Majesty's Inspectorate replied, 'to get off it' is now apocryphal, but there remain too many children ploughing their way through turgid and unstimulating material.

The problem with the insistence on phonic instruction as the most important element in the reading process that can be found in the 1993 rewrite of the National Curriculum is that it ignores the essential role of the context for reading and the importance of meaning making while substituting rote learning and de-contextualized drills. For example, the programmes of study at Key Stage 1 (five- to seven-year olds) emphasize word identification and recognition, information about words, grammatical structure and meaning, as if these skills are acquired outside the reading process and can be directly taught. The whole vocabulary of these revised orders implies direct instruction. For example it is suggested that reading activities should include (DFE, 1993):

- identifying and using a comprehensive range of letters and sounds (including combinations of letters, blends and digraphs) and paying specific attention to their use in the formation of words;
- attention to syllables in longer words;

- recognizing alliteration, sound patterns and rhyme;
- experimenting with sound–symbol relationships in their own writing.

The argument against such a programme of study is not that children do not need to use these skills in making sense of print but that the emphasis of the orders has been placed on direct instruction at the expense of purposeful reading experience. This is particularly noticeable in the key stage-related advice where it is suggested:

> Pupils whose pre-school literacy has been less extensive will need more emphasis on the initial stages of reading, including the alphabet, and teaching specifically designed to raise their awareness of sounds and patterns of sounds as a preparation for phonic work.

Second, and subordinated to the emphasis on phonics, is the suggestion that 'They will also require an extensive introduction to books and stories'. All research into early literacy, as for example Wells' Bristol study (1985), shows that the latter is the essential feature of success in learning to read and in reversing the order of importance the new orders seriously threaten the nature of the early reading curriculum. Moreover, it is much more difficult to stimulate children's interest in reading once a pattern of failure or boredom has been established. It was in the light of the media's emphasis on an unsubstantiated claim of a nationwide reading failure that Nottinghamshire Advisory and Inspection Service and Educational Psychology Service conducted the countywide survey (1991), in order to produce a more detailed picture of reading in its schools at the time when reports of the first National Tests of seven-year olds' reading were made public in 1991. A questionnaire was sent to all primary, infant and first schools and this was followed up by an in-depth survey of 18 selected schools through interviews with teachers, parents and pupils. The survey uncovered no evidence to support press assertions of a widespread lack of confidence amongst teachers of their ability to teach reading effectively. On the contrary the Nottinghamshire Advisory and Inspection Service and Educational Psychology Service Survey (1991) reported that:

> Teachers universally gave reading the highest priority in the primary curriculum and most schools were confident that, apart from minor details, they were making the right provision. The overriding intention of most teachers was to support children in achieving a minimum baseline of competence.

The evidence both from the HMI and this local authority study, however, did suggest that many children's access to wider reading materials in school was limited and therefore their expectations of what constituted reading was shaped by this experience. The Nottinghamshire survey reported that,

> [Children] were less strong in the range of reading strategies they were able to use and there was a general neglect of non-fiction and the associated information retrieval skills

and that non-fiction was much less popular; in one or two instances children even suggested that they 'hated' information books.

In a presentation of the results to the local education authority, which summed up the effectiveness of Nottinghamshire primary schools' reading policies, it was concluded that:

> if effectiveness means 'children could handle reasonably well the reading one would expect of children of this age', then the standard is satisfactory or better and if 'effectiveness' means willing to read, then the standard is high, but if effectiveness means 'able to choose and read a range of reading material for a range of purposes,' then the standard is less than satisfactory across the whole range of children.

Most writers about reading do so from their own particular perspective. Educational psychologists tend to treat reading failure as a pathology with specific elements of perception and cognition that need treatment, the emphasis is on diagnosis and remediation rather than development, pleasure and purposeful activity. What has been deduced about reading from the struggles of children with learning difficulties is generalized to the population as a whole so that all children are required to practise sounds and plod through graded readers long after they are ready to read independently or for a specific task-related purpose. There is little mention in their work of the power of story or the imagination; learning to read is seen as a desired skill that can be broken down into a series of teachable sub-skills. On the other hand, specialists with their past education rooted in English Literature, like Margaret Meek, bring to their work an utter conviction that 'committed readers and writers help children to read and write because they know what these processes are good for'. They base their arguments on the pleasure that is to be found mainly in the reading of fiction because of their own rich experience of books and authors. In choosing fiction for children they tend to draw on an understanding of the child that they have been in describing the pleasures they find in each text. Their emphasis on narrative fiction as the prime medium for teaching reading strikes chords particularly with teachers of English at the secondary level who share this belief in personal fulfilment through engagement with powerful writing. Not everybody, however, shares the English specialist's enthusiasm for fictional narrative in book form, or is convinced of the centrality of imaginative fiction to their lives. For some of the pupils in my survey the experience of reading in school remained a dutiful slog, rather than a pleasure.

> 'The most books I read at my old school were fiction things. The teacher read fiction things a lot. One thing about reading there I disliked was if you did not like a book you still had to read it.'
>
> Boy, age 12

> 'I like to read books like *The Lost Vampire*. I did not like to read books in the school library. It was quiet in there and there were not many good books. Our teacher read some books to us but they were not very good.'
>
> Boy, age 11

'My parents think that if I read more I would be a better reader than I really am and my mum says that the only thing I read in the week is *Big* magazine and the television page from the paper.'

Girl, age 11

When narrative does engage such children's interest it is more often in the form of a televisual or film medium. Children, who have not been attracted to books while learning to read, need alternative strategies for motivating their reading other than the promise that a book will be pleasurable.

In the early stages of the National Oracy and Writing Projects, the researchers began by asking children about their views of the writing they produced in school. The data collected helped them to focus on key areas for development in the writing curriculum. It is a long time since any wide-ranging survey attempted to find out what children choose to read and how this generation perceives themselves as readers in school. In the following section I intend to draw on the experiences of my sample of 11-year-old children to identify some of the longer-term consequences of a model of reading based on pleasure and individual choice and to identify the kinds communities of readers currently being built in our schools.

Implications for classroom development

1 The overwhelming evidence from both independent research and the School Inspectorate is that mixed methods of teaching reading are the most effective. No single method ensures success for all children and all children need access to a wide range of genres and written formats to understand the purposes and audiences for print. There is therefore a need for schools to broaden their book stocks, providing a wide range of non-fiction as well as narrative fiction for all classes.

2 Phonic awareness can be developed effectively in a programme that sees reading and writing as mutually supportive and draws children's attention to the structure of words in the course of their own composition. Children's early picture stories are rich in features that develop phonemic awareness through rhyme, alliteration, assonance and repeated syntactic frames.

3 Attempts to enforce the teaching of phonics as the central aspect of early reading are unhelpful because they ignore the importance of meaning and purpose in the initial stages of reading and substitute de-contextualized drill.

4 Many older junior children would continue to benefit from a whole-language approach to reading where print is seen as part of the environment in creative play or role playing.

5 Teachers of older children need to have a clear picture of the kind of reading children have experienced in the earlier phases of their education and the ways they have been taught to deal with unknown words. They

should aim to form a better picture of each child's reading abilities and preferences by keeping more detailed records.

6 Children's language experience is a valuable starting point for creating both class books and individual readers. Familiarity with the meaning makes the stories highly predictable and enables beginners and those experiencing difficulty to gain in fluency. Teachers need to be aware, however, of the significant differences between written and spoken forms of the language. They need to ensure children experience sufficiently demanding books to broaden the range of written registers they encounter.

7 Children need an early immersion in the language of well-told stories and children's poetry to develop a knowledge of written conventions. Early picture books scaffold children's learning through structural devices of pattern and repetition. Stories are both memorable and predictable and invite the active participation of the learner in shared reading sessions. Poems help to develop prediction skills and encourage phonemic awareness of through rhyme, alliteration and onomatopoeia.

8 Children who are not fluent readers by the middle years need to encounter stimulating reading material and related language experiences rather than being restricted to repetitive practice of phonic skills alone, although these will form part of any reading recovery strategy.

9 Good liaison between stages is vital if children are to build on the work already achieved and move towards more advanced reading. Individual records should include details of how children tackle a range of texts as well as exactly what and how much they read.

10 Records should include details of children's reading strategies and the range of reading materials they have used both in and out of schools.

2 The pleasures of reading

Pupils should become increasingly independent as readers. Reading should be promoted as an enjoyable activity, with sufficient time made available for it.

(DFE, 1993)

One of the major reasons teachers have always given for encouraging children to read fiction in school is the conviction that, because reading is pleasurable in itself, stories encourage children to become fluent readers and help to establish the literacy skills that they can carry through into adult life. Teachers therefore expect extensive and wide-ranging reading of fiction to produce children who read fluently and without effort and who will ultimately be equally at ease with a physics textbook as with a Shakespeare play.

In a recent account (Wade, 1990: 58) of how her own school set out to engage the parents in a support role for their children's reading development in the early years, Chris Burman, a Birmingham advisory teacher, identifies just such reasons for working with stories. Her conviction is that stories have the ability to excite children's interest in reading and give children the message that learning to read is enjoyable, purposeful and meaningful.

Shared-reading experiences give children the message that learning to read is enjoyable, purposeful and meaningful. They find out at the very beginning that books are worthwhile and have an important part to play in their lives. Shared-reading encourages positive attitudes; the reading and enjoyment of the stories is seen as its own reward. There is no hint of competition or the need for extrinsic reward; no need to 'please mummy or teacher' or to 'get on to a higher book'. Sharing stories in this way emphasises that reading is a sociable activity, for when children read exciting stories they want to share what they have found with others. Even the quietest child is stimulated to talk, express feelings and ideas.

One of the difficulties with this starting point for the teacher is in determining exactly what kinds of stories will effect this transformation and particularly, as children grow older, which books they themselves choose as a 'good story' as opposed to the books that are recommended as pleasurable by their teachers. The question becomes even more complex in the later stages of education where tastes become far more disparate and the range of possible reading is very much wider. It is the divergence of individual reading interests which raises the question of how far a teacher should allow children's existing tastes to determine what will be read in school.

The issue is further confused by the role of imaginative literature in education. The combination of pleasure with fiction, as the hook to draw children into reading in the early years, may suggest an absence of rigorous work and so reading activities may always be used to fill in free time, whereas the concept of 'literature', the form in which reading is presented at the older end of the school system, brings with it an obligation to study and perhaps even memorise, works that are less accessible to the younger reader. Part of this second assumption when books are labelled as literary, is an accompanying belief that exposure to certain kinds of writing is in itself beneficial. The Bullock Committee reflected teachers' views that literature 'helps shape the personality, refine the sensibility, sharpen the critical intelligence. In Britain the tradition of literature teaching is one which aims at personal and moral growth' (DES, 1975: 125).

The dichotomy that exists between the rigours of study and the pleasures of print have been presented as polarities in the act of reading from the beginnings of recorded commentary. Horace, one of the Western world's first recorded literary critics, suggested that an author's intentions in writing should be to give profit or delight to the reader, qualifying this with the suggestion that it is the elders who seek profit from reading while the youngsters look only for its pleasures. He further suggests that a writer who can give delight while at the same time instructing his reader or audience wins everybody's approbation. That both these concepts are lurking at the back of teachers' minds when they consider reading is illustrated in a chapter by Nelms and Zancanella (1990) entitled 'The Experience and Study of Literature,' which describes an American enquiry in which undergraduate English majors, about to enter a teaching programme, were required to list the associations that cluster round the concept of 'literature'. Some of the terms supplied, particularly by mature students had roots in 'a deep sense of personal pleasure', with ideas clustering round terms like 'exciting', 'adventures', 'bedtime', 'cuddling' and 'recreation'; other students focused on the 'mechanics of critical terminology' such as 'epic', 'realism', 'setting', theme, etc. The authors of the paper concluded:

> These tensions or 'conflicts' seem to be specific examples of larger conflicts in the study and teaching of literature – between the ideas of the New Critics and the ideas of reader response theorists; between wanting readers to read 'good' literature and simply wanting them to read; between what Rosenblatt calls efferent readings and aesthetic readings – literature as information or literature as exploration.

In English schools the literature or reading curriculum, particularly for younger age groups, is not at present as closely structured or prescribed as most American schemes of work. English is based on a holistic approach to language use and development. However, a similar tension between what children choose to read for themselves and the books prescribed for them is currently being created in the practice of the National Curriculum. There is requirement for all children in the later stages of education to 'study' and 'evaluate' texts. For children in the middle years the suggestions include 'some classic poetry' and 'figurative language both in poetry and prose' and for secondary pupils, Shakespeare and some pre-twentieth century literature, which reflects the 'literary heritage', are imposed. Children's fiction and literature have always been uneasy companions in schools, without any clear demarcation of where one ends and the other emerges. There also exists a long list of children's writers who have been awarded literary prizes and gained adult approval but who have been read by very few children from choice. What is agreed is that politicians, parents and teachers all expect children to learn to read fluently and become skilled in working with print. What they can not agree on, however, is what should be read, how books should be presented to children or even when and where reading should take place. This has culminated in the ludicrous strategy of the now disbanded Secondary Assessment and Examination Council, in the school year 1992–3, collating a national anthology of set texts for 14-year olds which contains only fragments of works recognized as 'literary' or 'worth studying' with the inclusion not only of Shakespeare but also of Samuel Johnson, Chaucer, Dickens and Wordsworth. Very few of these texts would feature in a 14-year-old's assessment of what they enjoyed reading; indeed, very few of them are texts which their teachers would consider to be appropriate for the full ability range, yet these are texts which have been selected to test children's response for an attainment target which stresses (DFE, 1993: 40):

> Some texts should be studied, but the main emphasis should be the encouragement of wider reading by independent, responsive and enthusiastic readers.

'Responsive' and 'enthusiastic' both suggest that reading should be predicated on personal interest, yet little has been done to discover exactly what it is that children willingly read. We have few up-to-the-minute research details of children's attitudes to the reading they undertake either voluntarily or at school, and the national picture is blurred by a press that suggests that current teaching of reading has been almost entirely through a medium of 'real books' when inspectors and advisory teachers know the true picture in schools is very different from this.

It is now over twenty years since Frank Whitehead completed the nationwide survey of children's leisure reading (Whitehead *et al.*, 1974) which alerted English teachers to the steady decline in their pupils' voluntary reading as they progressed through the secondary school. Whitehead's team conducted the national survey by a questionnaire which sampled children in three age groups,

10, 12 and 14, using 188 schools and 7800 children to ensure the results were representative. One of the major findings was that in a large number of the schools which participated, the teachers did not see the reading of full books as one of their teaching concerns. Instead, the report highlighted the prevalence at that time of work in English based on extracts rather than whole books, recommending that

> . . . if the development of wide or independent reading is a central or important goal of English teaching (and surely this should be axiomatic) then this objective is most effectively attained by a concentration in English lessons upon the reading of 'real' books (novels, stories and other complete prose books) rather than the study of extracts.

I would argue that it is Whitehead's work that has been instrumental in creating a climate in secondary English departments for fostering pupils' independent reading as a school-based activity. This manifested itself through English teachers at the secondary phase taking a keener interest in children's books and teenage fiction, as well as, or later instead of, relying on staples of the canonical school reading diet, such as *Jim Davies*, *Kidnapped*, *David Copperfield* and *Ivanhoe*, used for reading practice round the class, supplemented by chapters set for reading homework.

These practices were replaced, at a time when departmental allowances were more generous, with class libraries and book boxes which reflected the range and diversity of children's tastes and abilities at each stage of development. A good book box selection for 12–13-year olds (Y8) would range from sophisticated picture stories such as those of Raymond Brigg's *Gentleman Jim* or Russell Hoban's *Captain Najork and His Team of Hired Sportsmen* to adult reading such as Bronte's *Jane Eyre* and Orwell's *Animal Farm*, while including a wide range of works by a large number of acknowledged children's writers such as Philippa Pearce, Betsy Byars, Bernard Ashley and Leon Garfield. In the secondary school, particularly in their first two years, pupils were given time in class to choose from their own interests and to express personal opinions about what they were reading in diaries or reading records. At the same time, new class readers, which reflected the pupils' developing literary interests became the central focus for the curriculum, providing much of the stimulus for other activities in writing and drama.

The success of these twin drives in the resourcing of the English classroom can be measured by the later movement in educational publishing away from coursework books containing small extracts and manageable poems, followed by suggestions for writing and some more discursive questions, as for example Nancy Martin's *Come Down and Startle* or Clements, Dixon and Stratta's *Things Being Various* to series of children's fiction selected by a specialist editor like Geoff Fox, and photo-copiable teachers' files of suggested approaches, such as the Macmillan '*M*' books (1990) based on the children's books published in its Windmill series.

This is not to say that course books have completely disappeared from the market, but the emphasis of the wider reading model is reflected in their greater use of contemporary poetry and short stories and is signalled by stock cupboards which contain multiple copies of books by children's writers. The model for many secondary English departments is to base a good deal of written work in English on such a class reader where specific features of narrative and language can be explored together while providing some class time for children's own independent reading. However, there are key pointers in Whitehead *et al.*'s study (1977) that suggest that to begin to focus on independent reading at 11+ may well be too late for many children. Reading needs to be given the kind of attention that will carry readers into more and more challenging texts on their own at an earlier stage. The question posed at the end of the survey ('Does the reading of poor quality books at 10+ form a foundation upon which better reading tastes develop at later ages, or does it lead more typically to a loss of interest in what books have to offer?') has not yet been adequately answered. Research into children's reading habits has been left to individual institutions and so it is hard to form a clear picture of current national habits and trends in popular tastes. Reading fiction is firmly embedded in the secondary school curriculum but is the same true of the period preceding transfer, when children's reading habits need to be established? Much of the evidence that exists from the APU (1988), HMI reports, (DES, 1991) and the Nottingham survey (Nottinghamshire Advisory and Inspection Service and Educational Psychology Service, 1991) suggests it is not. At the end of the primary phase it is hard to point to work that is particularly focused on reading development if by that I mean purposeful individual or group activity directing pupils to make sense of a work of fiction or poetry. Books are more often shared as stories read aloud by the teacher as relaxation or time-fillers at the end of a busy morning or afternoon's work, and the majority of time given up to individual reading is left to children's own choice. It is the largely unexamined emphasis on the effectiveness of reading for pleasure as the only policy for developing readers in the middle years that I wanted to explore in more detail.

If there is, as it has been suggested by the French critic, Roland Barthes (1977), a universal appetite for stories and narrative is to be found in cultural artefacts as disparate as 'myth, legend, fable, tale, novella, epic, history, tragedy, drama, comedy, mime, stained glass windows, cinema, comics, news items, conversations' because narrative is 'international, transhistorical, transcultural . . . simply there like life itself', then twenty years on from the last national survey of reading behaviour, what we can say with complete certainty is there are many more ways of satisfying this particular human need for story than those provided in print. In 1974, Whitehead identified the major competitor for children's attention in their leisure periods as television, then accessible only at the time of transmission and with a very limited range of programmes specifically appealing to children. Today, not only have the number of television channels increased, but in addition, video recording technology makes films and recorded programmes available in many homes for 24 hours a day. Added to this, a large proportion of children have a television set in their own room so their personal access to visual entertainment is unlimited. Computer programmes with sophisticated graphics now entice the operator into fictional worlds where quest-like narratives with fantasies of heroic encounters with warriors and monsters can be acted out on the screen. The possession of a joy stick gives the young participant control over the progress and outcome of a particular adventure. Nearly all computer games, whatever their origin, are promoted on the strength of their ability to create excitement. For example, one home-computer club, which provides programmes for a popular computer, typically advertises a new game in the following terms:

> Is your life lacking a bit of excitement? Then why not practice your archery with Robin Hood, control the wrath of the demon, take part in some of the most vivid simulations around, play tennis at professional level band then put on your suit to do your home accounts.

A reviewer describes a new game as a personal adventure in the form of a narrative (*Amiga Format*, Future Publishers, November 1992):

> As he slept in his homely hole on Putty moon, Putty began to dream about his old Grandpa . . .
> 'Ee you must remember as well as I do young Putty. The moon used to be a quiet place, and our people lived in peace and harmony. Until that is the evil wizard Dazzledaze, and his cohort [sic] Dweezil the cat decided to pick on us . . .'
> It quickly becomes apparent that the Bots are not only harmless aliens but also inordinately stupid. How can they build a huge tower from Zid to the Moon when they can't find their way back to the spaceship, I don't know?
> All seems serene and gentle until. Aaargh, the second level really drops you in at the deep end with loads of horrible aliens and three Bots to save. The Terminator Carrot [sic] makes his first appearance here and is instantly likeable even though he's trying to pump you full of lead. Punch him to reveal a crying baby.

The narrative genre is instantly recognisable as that of a quest but the added attraction for the gamester is the active nature of the participation offered. Unlike the written description of the action in the magazine, the narrative of computer games is conveyed in a visual form and the youngest players can quickly become adept at predicting outcomes of moves made in the quest formats on which many of the programmes are based. Young readers also have their needs met by a new generation of computer programmes described as 'living books'. The computer screen presents the child with what looks like a conventional story book except that the characters speak the words displayed and when the mouse is used to click on specific sections of the illustration unusual and amusing things happen – a whale blows a jet of water from the ocean, hermit crabs perform a little dance while in the background a fisherman catches an ocean liner on his hook.

Many of the children in the survey reported a preference for adventure stories, and their continuing addiction to the recently up-dated Enid Blyton coupled to a new interest in Steve Jackson's *Fantasy Adventures* books support this. Adventure is readily catered for by the computer games market. Moreover, the technology already exists which will transform children into the physical protagonists of such worlds through 'virtual reality', giving a whole new dimension to the concept of being lost in a story.

Even Whitehead's argument for the superiority of the book as a more readily available source of personal gratification is thrown into question by the new technology. The aptly named Japanese *Game Boy* (apt because owners consist largely of boys between the ages of 8 and 14) provides a pocket version of highly sophisticated adventure games for the adolescent hooked on computers. It is exactly the size of a paperback book and has a wide variety of arcade and adventure games available. Although the interaction these games offer does not provide opportunities for the self-discovery and self-realization which most English teachers accept as an integral and central component in any conception of education, it does allow the players to build up a store of narrative frameworks and to exercise the skills of prediction that are part of the experience of story for younger pupils.

Because there is so much more competition for children's leisure time it is even more axiomatic that sound habits of reading, coupled with opportunities to make use of and reflect on what has been read, should be an essential part of children's structured learning. The middle years are particularly important in establishing attitudes that allow children to become part of a larger community of readers, and in creating an expectation that reading is an essential aspect of their learning strategies. Teachers need therefore to be asking themselves what criteria they should be using to select the books that children will encounter at this critical stage in their learning and how much mediation is required to foster response. All available research data confirm that this is the time when readers are confirmed as life-long addicts of the pleasure and new challenges of literature or when the habit can lose its hold on even the most proficient de-coder.

In a recent essay, Jack Ousbey, who devoted much of his career as a Local Authority Inspector to promoting work with fiction in school, outlines the challenge facing teachers who are committed to the role of the imagination in education. He has consistently argued for the choice of books which 'nourish and sustain the imagination' and supported their promotion in schools. In his latest writing (Ousbey, 1992) he warns against the growing utilitarian bias of the curriculum that works to undermine the commitment to creative involvement in literature.

The trouble with words like 'pleasure', 'enjoyment', 'humour', 'celebration', however, is that they do not fit easily into the discourse of current educational debate . . . Wise teachers, like wise parents, have to redefine and defend the place of creative activities and imaginative experiences, not as option but as entitlements.

Because any criticism of strategies for reading development that are based on 'individual reading for pleasure' might be construed as a call for a return to more instrumental learning, through comprehension passages for example, it is vital that teachers think carefully about the issues involved in structuring reading experience in the classroom. The major task in the crucial middle years of schooling is first to nourish the reading habit and secondly to ensure pupils encounter books which challenge their understanding and stretch their imaginations. If certain sections of the age group are having the pleasure of the text opened up to them by genres teachers find difficult to accept (as is the case with the romance or 'teen' novel for girls; Willinsky and Hunford, 1993: 88–92), then it seems counterproductive to close this option down. What is important is that teachers understand existing personal tastes in reading in order to build on them. To do this it is important to find out what stories children say they enjoy and determine how far their understanding of literature is broadened by the books they choose for themselves. These were questions I could only answer with confidence by getting a clearer picture of the way children viewed their own reading development and their priorities in selecting books to read for themselves. It is therefore with the views of the children in their final year of primary school that I want to explore in more detail the nature of choice and personal pleasure.

In the 1970s, by far the most frequently named author in Whitehead's survey was Enid Blyton and much the same holds true for the children in my study, who were interviewed during their last year in primary school. Enid Blyton's combination of fast-moving plot with predictable outcomes and stereotyped characters facilitates both reading and comprehension. Go to the children's shelves of any bookshop and you will find large numbers of her books in their re-vamped paperback versions. For 10- and 11-year olds she is still the most frequently named writer and is usually mentioned alongside 'adventure' as being the most interesting kind of reading. She is most frequently cited by girls but is also mentioned by some of the boys. Roald Dahl and Judy Blume are then equally second most popular, though Judy Blume is seen as mainly a writer of 'girls' books while Dahl is read equally by both boys and girls. In general, then, children choose to read popular authors and return to the same ones for a guaranteed pleasure. They enjoy the 'readerly' text which confirms their expectations of what they have already read. Their individual reading choice is usual unadventurous and follows gendered paths. However, when I looked at the pupils' responses in more detail it became obvious that the school's methods of promoting books made a major difference to whether proven favourites were the only authors that the junior pupils could name and discuss. Teachers who were knowledgeable about books and prepared to make reading a priority could influence a whole class's reading. This in effect repeats

Whitehead's findings that in the schools where children recorded reading well above average numbers of books over the period of the survey, there were one or more teachers who were enthusiastic about reading and promoted the use of books in school.

To illustrate the difference, I shall compare the replies of two 11-year-old girls. The first, Shairon was a pupil at a inner-city school with a large ethnic mix. Her teacher described his strategy to promote reading as allowing the class a free choice of books brought in from home and school. Very little attention, however was given to matching children to particular books although they were frequently reminded to choose books that are appropriate for their reading 'standard'. Shairon was identified by her teacher as an average reader. She declared that she loved books and story books in particular. She explained that she used to like Enid Blyton and Roald Dahl but she was beginning to find them too young for her, and could find nothing to substitute for them in the school library:

> 'I like reading adventure books. When I was little I used to like reading all the *Famous Five* ones. I like a mystery but they're too easy for me now to read and I've read them all loads of times, over. I buy some from W.H. Smiths and I get some from the library.'

The 'free choice' allowed her in her school reading offered little solution to her problem of where to look for pleasure in reading beyond Enid Blyton. Instead of being given new challenging books in school, she relied on buying books for herself or borrowing from the local library.

The concept of free choice in her class also seemed somewhat illusory and restrictions on what was considered appropriate created difficulties for a developing reader: 'We have free choice but the teacher always says you've got to make sure it's up to your standard.' When asked how she did that, Shairon explained she did not really know but relied on looking at what the writing was like. Smaller print was her single criteria for more advanced reading.

Other factors were also at play in her classroom that militated against the development of strong commitments to books, although reading was a regular feature of the classroom and everybody was expected to read in class for half an hour after dinner. She describes the session as something that involves assessment and which is not always well received by her classmates.

Shairon: We just read for half an hour in class and sometimes the teacher will say, 'Come and read to me' and he'll write how he thinks you are.
Interviewer: And do you enjoy that time to read?
Shairon: Yes. Some people say that it's boring; they call me 'teacher's pet' for reading, but I like it.

In contrast, Helen's school provided a more supportive framework for personal choice. Her school was located out of town in a newish housing estate with a largely white working-class catchment area. The school was one of the few in Nottinghamshire's survey (Nottinghamshire Advisory and Inspection Service and Educational Psychology Services 1991) whose reading policy was based on a full commitment to reading with 'real books' and had well-stocked class libraries in all the classrooms as well as a central library area and a well-stocked bookshop. In the infant school, children were encouraged to read from a wide selection of new picture books and every child in the school had a reading wallet and took books home to share with parents. Helen had been given much more indirect help in the choice of books by her school. Her initial reading interests are similar to Shairon's but her teacher's engagement with the books his class reads and his commitment to sharing his own favourites with the class has moved her on to other kinds of reading.

'I like sort of adventure stories and Enid Blyton's books I like the most, I think. I like some Judy Blume books and Betsy Byars. I think I have got some at home and then I get some off the library bus that comes round. At the moment I'm reading one that a student teacher brought in. I've just forgotten what it's called, but it's all different stories in it. I think I've had a lot of Judy Blume ones, that's how I got to like her, and Betsy Byars I've had a lot of, and teachers read those sort of books to us as well. That's how I got to know them. I think that's all the ones that have been in school.

Joan Aitken's good because she does more like different stories in one book, so they're short stories you can read. Then there's Betsy Byars and Judy Blume and Enid Blyton that do longer stories but keep you interested, whereas some of the authors write long books but they get boring towards the end. But others keep interesting all the way through.'

Helen, who was also an 'average' reader in her teacher's estimation, had been encouraged to keep a careful record of the books she had read in the past two years. Her reading record book was arranged alphabetically and there was a summary document at the back, whereby looking at filled in squares she could see how many books she had read in a particular month. When asked about her reading interests she looked through this record to remind herself of the books she had enjoyed and the reasons for her choice. She found a range of names she had not included in her list of favourite books but which had all provided good reads. These included Vivien Alcock, Margaret Mahy, Philippa Pearce and Betsy Byars, all authors whom teachers would encourage their pupils to read.

The reasons she gave for her personal preferences were very similar to the explanation given by Shairon for the books she selected.

'Well they're [the children in Enid Blyton stories] always going on different adventures, when they don't mean to, just fall into adventures like. And then they follow them until they catch who's doing things.'

Helen

'They keep me in suspense and make me want to read on. Because sometimes I read before I go to bed and I'll be just going to sleep and I'll be thinking about my book and have to get up again and start reading.'

Shairon

Shairon, however, has no record of the books she has encountered in school; she has kept a reading record in the past but the habit has 'slipped away'.

> 'We just used to write the title of the book and write down the date and what page we started on and the page that we finished on.'

Similarly, when asked who was a good reader in her class, Helen confidently named a group of girls whom she described as sharing books with each other and recommending them to her. She explained that she knew that they were good readers because they read books quickly and liked to talk about them. In Helen's class, time was given for exchanging views on reading and there was a common acceptance that this was part of the school's culture. Shairon was much more hesitant about naming her classes' 'good readers'. She suggested that reading was something that was not particularly valued by her class:

> 'I don't know [who is a good reader]. I don't think – people like say. I don't think they really like reading very much, but they can read well. Yeah, they can read well but I wouldn't say that they enjoyed reading.'

Helen and Shairon expressed similar attitudes to their individual reading and shared common popular tastes. For each them the main point of reading was to solve the enigmas created by the adventures in the readerly texts which always gave them what they expected. Both claimed to read widely at home, and the main difference in their experience of reading arose from what had been actively provided for them by their schools.

Reading was an important part of Helen's everyday classroom experience. She had been given space to share her reading interests with both her teacher and her classmates and used this to extend her range and knowledge of authors and variety of story types. Reading and writing were closely interlinked and she had been working on a class project to write the kind of story which people her age enjoyed. Her positive attitude to reading in class was mirrored by her classmate, Matthew, who had joined the school in the middle of Y5 (age nine). His experience of reading in his previous school had not been so positive. He described learning to read on what appeared to be a series of reading scheme books scornfully:

> 'They weren't very interesting. Just like another chapter of a little story, just one page books and things like that. So I always used to read at home because I've got plenty of me own books. I read magazines and Turtle books and things like that.'

He also described his mother's role as important in helping him find books and hearing him read at this stage in his learning, but in this school his mother's role had been replaced by his classroom teacher's influence, particularly the way his new teacher shared whole books with the class. Matthew reported particularly enjoying the times when the teacher read.

> 'Well it depends how they're read and who reads them. If a kid reads them they don't like get the real expression. But if a grown-up reads them then it's twice as good.'

Gareth who was Shairon's classmate also spoke about the shared class book, *White Fang*, which he could recall and recount in detail. His teacher has described him as a good reader and he talked with enthusiasm about enjoying books, particularly stories of detection and mystery. He did not, however, find much to engage his interest in the class library:

> 'Lots of them are just like – most of them are just right little thin books, we've not got a lot of big books like the one I'm reading now. They're only about that – centimetre thick. But the one I'm reading that's about two centimetres. If it's not a thick book I'll get through them too quickly and soon I'd have read all the books in the class.'

Despite his enthusiasm for reading he was unable to recall any author or give a particular title that he had enjoyed other than *White Fang* and the latter had been impressed on his memory by a video version shown to the whole class.

The thickness of the books they read was a major concern of all the children. In the absence of any other criteria for judging progress, it is the one they use to assess the difficulty of books and their own, and other people's ability as readers. They also placed great emphasis on the importance of completing the book they were reading in school whether they were enjoying it or not. Matthew claimed that others would 'snitch' if they noticed someone skipping pages in their book. Most agreed that the better readers were those who were reading the thicker books. As is suggested by research evidence of pupils' attitudes to reading published by the APU in 1987, boys were less likely to make a spontaneous choice of fiction and more often mentioned factual writing when asked specifically about enjoyment. Tim mentioned 'adventure' books as his favourite, but these turned out to be not story book adventures but factual accounts of famous explorations. As he explained:

> 'I like to read books that you can really get into like adventure books, because I'm doing this topic and I've got this gi-normous book and I think there's 100 adventures . . . everybody is doing a certain topic and I'm doing the Antarctic when Scott went an' all that and I'm doing my research at home. Me gran's got me an information booklet.'

Tim had a persuasive explanation as to why information books were more important than stories:

> 'I can keep up the data with my friend and you can tell them about what happened. But with like other books, I mean they're all the same, you can't really tell them. You can tell them about the basic story but it's not like something to say, it's like a personal reading thing.'

The other books that Tim mentioned owning included a pocket atlas, some encyclopedias given to him by his dad, comic books and some Ladybird books from an adventure series. In Tim's closest community of readers it is information that is valued and which makes the links with others. Reading of fiction is more personal and therefore less valued. He does, however, do some private reading in school and likes Roald Dahl, particularly for the illustrations. Tim also liked the Usborne information books in the school library, describing his enjoyment of the mixture of pictures and short summarized information together with puzzles and the other practical things to do.

Jennie was in the same class as Tim but her priorities in reading were very different from his. She read Judy Blume and *Sweet Valley High* books and liked some of Enid Blyton stories. She enjoyed stories about 'everyday' things best and often swapped her books with her friends: 'We usually say whether they're good or which you don't like and which bit you like best.' When she began to recount details in the books she had found most interesting she talked about 'going out to discos', 'doing homework at the last minute', 'keeping up with fashion' and 'friends drifting apart and making it up again'. These things she took to be the stuff of everyday life. She preferred to bring the books she read in school from home, sharing them with her friends. She found most non-fiction books 'boring' and the least interesting thing she can imagine for her reading was 'books about inventions or something'. She has however used reference books to write a project on animals although she has found it hard to get relevant information from the school library. Her friends, all girls, share her tastes in fiction. The patterns of reading described by Jennie and Tim work to reinforce gender expectations and confirm their existing understanding of appropriate roles so that Tim's experience of fiction has done nothing to draw him into literature and Jennie's addiction to the kind of popular fiction that creates a cosy world of personal relationships and romance has little to say of the wider sphere of the world at large.

In all the primary schools except one, there seemed to be an unquestioning acceptance by the staff that children would develop as readers, if given sufficient space and time to read books that interested them. What surprised me was how few of the pupils, except in the case of Helen and her classmates, were engaged in reading the kind of books that make their way onto recommended reading lists for the age range. Although on one hand, freedom to select what you like to read creates a climate in which learners define their own interests and create their own reading communities on the other, it also serves to limit their reading experience. Just as an over-narrow interpretation of a language experience approach can limit the learner to those common spoken language structures and mundane experiences that come from a restricted lifestyle and imagination, so trusting the pupils' choice of reading may reinforce patterns that are comfortable but undemanding, repetitive and unchallenging, and which rely on formulaic plotting and unsubtle or empty characterization.

The point about the majority of stories that circulate freely amongst children is that although the titles change from generation to generation the plots remain predictable in both content and style. Children settle down and consume these books one after another knowing what to expect and their expectations are not challenged in any way; rather their prejudices are confirmed. Working-class life is always shown as mean and damaging, gypsies steal babies, school teachers are stupid, mums spoil the fun. This is not an argument for censoring children's reading in the way that some secondary English departments do, by limiting their choice of independent reading to approved fictional genres and authors and vetting material that comes from home. As Margaret Meek (1991: 146) is wont to reiterate, children require more 'positive invitations to read' rather than prohibitions and restrictions that further divide reading in school from the reading they choose to do from their own enthusiasms. Independent reading should be just that, free from too much interference and arranged for times when children find reading comfortable and pleasant. Meek also reminds us that Enid Blyton's writing gives children practice in sustained reading.

> Young readers know they can read when they can tackle a whole book on their own; they recognise how the author does it and seem to see through the words to the meaning. That is what Enid Blyton has taught generations of girls and some boys to understand because she always plays the game by the rules.

These rules include establishing friendship groups of pre-adolescent children and a dog, who have been freed from the observation and control of their parents. They are always given plenty of picnics with cake, chocolate and ginger beer and provided with a supporting cast of adult adversaries and slow-witted policemen to be outmanoeuvred and defeated. The adventures take place in idyllic settings by the sea or in the country where summer is perpetual and never rainy, and adventure always on hand. Meek suggests that in these stories young readers look for imaginary relationships and are 'trying out different kinds of companionship, perhaps of those whose lives seem to involve them in more risk-taking than their own'. What is also being taught is the generic features of text and the chronological pull of narrative that carries the reader through to the end and a final resolution. Donald Fry (1985) described how 12-year-old Karnail, new to secondary school and inexperienced in reading, gained confidence as he learned he could handle Enid Blyton's *Secret Seven* books. Fry argues that the series gives him 'context support' in that there are a series of expectations of what a story should be that will always be met for Karnail by a Blyton adventure. He is learning to consume texts and in the process gaining fluency.

Many teachers take the children's initial enjoyment of a book as the most important consideration and one junior teacher in a recent survey of popular fiction admitted to reading Enid Blyton to the class although the choice conflicted with her sense of what was appropriate classroom reading (Sarland, 1991: 9). It is a different matter however to be content with reading as consumption without offering something a little more challenging as a focus for reading in class. Teachers have traditionally been unhappy with children's addiction to Blyton without adequately theorizing what it is that causes their dissatisfaction. In fact, opposition to this writer in particular is so strong as to represent a significant factor in the organization of 'independent' reading.

Some schools include the whole range of her books in their class libraries to encourage reluctant or struggling readers whilst others ban their inclusion all together. What seems to be at stake in such debates is the status of popular fiction and the criteria schools should use when selecting of books for private reading.

The issue is clouded by a growing tendency to set the 'literary' qualities of writing and a book's importance in shaping the young reader's growing sensibility, against fiction with popular appeal that goes down well. The real problem is that the reading of fiction in this important stage of learning has been weighted with too many functions. On the one hand, because in the middle years, free reading has replaced the role of the reading schemes' supplementary readers, it is intended to serve as a five-finger exercise in a basic skill which will be used for more important purposes later. As the earlier authority on reading, Schonnell suggests in *The Psychology and Teaching of Reading* (1945), work should be 'planned to give maximum practice with material suitable to the children's reading ages' because 'We should always keep in mind the fact that reading is only a means to an end, that end being the understanding of the printed word.'

On the other hand, reading practice is expected to develop a love of reading in preparation for the literary responses which will form a major part of their secondary school experience of English. This is evident in the National Curriculum's early stress on the importance of studying plot and character and supporting their opinions by reference to specific passages (DFE, 1993: 34).

Guidance for this second stage of primary education includes a requirement that:

> Pupils should develop as enthusiastic and reflective readers. They should be encouraged to respond imaginatively to the plot, characters ideas and language in literature, to be able to refer to relevant passages or episodes to support their opinions and to evaluate the books they read in writing or discussion.

The example given for this Attainment Target is:

> After reading *Jabberwocky* by Lewis Carroll, decide whether they think the monsters are threatening, funny or absurd, basing their opinion on view of the invented vocabulary.

Much of what children say they choose to read for themselves is a repetition of light pleasurable reading or simple information that offers no fresh challenges or new ways of engagement with ideas or language. It seems increasingly important that teachers should be able to think through their responsibilities for developing children's reading, particularly in these crucial years and question whether children's independent reading can carry the weight of all this baggage on its own. One of the recurrent difficulties for teachers is deciding how to choose books for particular classes, or how they might influence the reading that pupils are asked to do voluntarily. The current emphasis in literary critical theory on the role of the reader as producer of meaning, rather than on the author's role as guarantor of the profit or delight on offer, has allowed readings of popular culture that are more engaging and illuminating than the texts themselves. However, the critical ability to read texts in this way, that is to tell stories about stories, depends on a developing understanding of textual strategies based on an increasing sophistication in reading in response to particular kinds of writing.

Wide reading, well managed, may very well bring about the kind of exposure to increasingly sophisticated texts that is at the heart of the secondary curriculum, but can unguided reading give all pupils sufficient insights into the variety of ways in which textual meaning is shaped? Unguided responses to story often rely on preference rather than an understanding of genre or any reference to a wider cultural frame. Inexperienced readers respond naively to stories that have been written in a particular cultural context when they are unaware of the genre expectations. For example, in a case study of 13-year-old readers, Robert Protherough describes how some pupils gave a limited response to particular literary effects because of their unfamiliarity with the kind of writing represented. The readers had been asked to comment on their response to a James Thurber story, *The Princess and the Tin Box*, in which the conventions of fairy tales are turned on their head. Princes have been invited to compete for the hand of the princess by offering her gifts. The princess turns down the handsome but poor prince and marries the one who brought her a sapphire and platinum jewel box. Protherough (1987) reports:

> Thirteen (mostly boys) all expressed their dislike of the ending in similar terms to those of eleven and twelve year olds: it was not a proper ending for a fairy tale, endings should be predictable, this was a shock and I don't like shocks . . . The rather smaller number who rated the story above average described the ending as a 'refreshing change' 'an interesting twist', 'unconventional', 'more true to life'.

Protherough then suggests that such 'stories of reading provide one way of discovering which pupils will be capable of responding to certain kinds of literary effect'. It may also be a better indicator of the kinds of stories that each group has been accustomed to reading. Thurber's stories are not fairy stories but parodies of that genre and teacher intervention might have alerted the whole class to this rather than working from an expectation that the humour would be self-evident. Although the girls' responses are more in keeping with the genre some of their projections into character and empathy with the situation as 'more true to life' are not as appropriate as is the understanding of how Thurber is twisting the tale to achieve a humorous effect. In other words, responses need to be informed by experience of how different narratives work. I found a similar lack of understanding of a story's ending when working with a class of 11-year olds reading the fable of a farmer who warmed a frozen rattle-snake and got bitten for his pains. Unfamiliar with the nature of a fable's

moral purpose the class found the ending difficult to accept. They were looking for truths about relationships or a conventional animal rescue story with
proper rewards for kindness, and needed to have the snake's cruel retort to the
farmer who accuses him of killing someone who has shown him kindness,
'nature is nature', explained to them.

Programmes of reading need to address the range of genre in which
stories appear, if pupils are to move away from judging everything on a truth-
to-experience basis. Books, after all, do not offer the same experiences as those
in the reality they frequently describe. Perhaps the most useful way of understanding the difference between story as a primary act of mind and the kind of
stories we meet in print, is to adopt the structuralist viewpoint of the differences between events as they happen in time and the narration which is the
textual ordering of these events. All children tell events as simple chronologically
sequenced stories; it is only exposure to other forms of narration that allows
these personal stories to be restructured and developed in more complex ways,
with different narrators, narrative 'frames', flashbacks and parallel plottings.
Most stories are not written in a simple linear form and familiarity with story
convention is therefore culturally constructed. A personal growth approach to
reading development can too readily lead to uncritical acceptance of a model of
reading which considers only children's current interests and offers no way
into more challenging texts.

The work of post-structuralist critics, and in particular the later work
of Roland Barthes, has helped to clarify the difference that exists between
the pleasures of a complex and challenging text which the reader rewrites
for herself in the process of creating meaning and that of the readerly text
which delivers the same kind of satisfaction time and time again in a different
package.

In *S/Z*, a rewriting of the short story, *Sarrasine* by Balzac, Barthes uncovers
the layers of meaning governed by what he terms 'codes', which are those
conventions of narrative built on a knowledge of other texts and other ways of
telling stories. Barthes' codes are not used to reveal a pre-existing structure but
show how readers draw upon its latent structuration, drawing on previous
cultural and literary knowledge. The important feature of the analysis for those
with an interest in the development of reading strategies is that the codes are
built up from Barthes understanding of how stories go, how actions build to
plots, mysteries (enigmas) are formulated and characters are constructed rather
than an interpretation of their meaning as direct representation of a piece of
lived experience. Barthes makes it clear that all acts of reading depend on
pulling together the connotations and associations built up from prior textual
experience of these ways of coding prior experience. For Barthes, a text can
never be a simple reflection of reality; rather it is 'a tissue of quotations drawn
from innumerable centres of culture' (Barthes, 1977). Further, Barthes suggests that the ultimate pleasure of reading is a mastery of these structurations
that allows the sophisticated reader room for play. This is an entirely different

concept of pleasure than that associated with recognizing in books a reflection of reality that leads on to personal growth.

In a recent book in this series, Peter Griffiths (1991) has drawn attention to an important contradiction latent in the Bullock Report's attitude to the place of literature in the curriculum, by unpicking a strand in the report that values children's unguided reading preferences as a means of personal resource:

> Children we are told derive enjoyment in this way, and also compensation for the difficulties of growing up

but he also highlights the report's expectation that teachers must introduce pupils to books

> where a complexity of relationships enlarges . . . understanding of the range of human possibilities.

Wider reading was the strategy suggested by the report as the way of resolving this duality. Griffiths comments (1991: 56–61):

> It is, I think, defensible to adopt a position of believing that as wide and as varied as possible an exposure to fiction will contribute to an understanding of narrative devices, to intellectual growth and emotional development. It is also possible to adopt another position . . . in which a structured exposure to narrative devices of gradually increasing complexity forms at least one organising principle of the literature curriculum. Bullock appears to marshal a body of evidence for the latter argument, but to be deeply committed to the former one.

I think it is possible to see the same duality at work in the provision for children's reading from the middle years. The belief implicit in the emphasis on reading built on personal choice is that exposure will ensure growth of a more sophisticated understanding of story form, but the English curriculum at the second stage in education begins to expect a more considered and reflective response for which most unguided reading leaves many pupils poorly prepared.

There is a further dilemma associated with the choice of books for the classroom in the middle years. An emphasis on specifically children's fiction, like the stories of authors such as Betsy Byars, Penelope Lively and Gene Kemp can strike some of the children in the 10–13 age group as too juvenile and undemanding, whilst allowing a totally free choice can leave readers on a superficially sophisticated, but textually unchallenging level. Christine, for example, in her second interview, in the secondary school, age 12, remarks:

> 'Sometimes I wish that I could be with the second year because I like some of the work they do. They read books for their age group and I like reading books above my age group. I don't like reading books like *Moomin Papa*, I don't like those. Some of the books I want to read, it says fourth years only, because they think the first years wouldn't want to read them. You have to bring a note from your mother to say that she lets you read those books. I sometimes find that a bit annoying because lots of children in the first year enjoy those kind of books. There was one where robots take over the world, just like a future book. The

robots blocked all your minds and they made you forget old times. Maybe it had violent bits where there are people getting punished . . . it wasn't very violent – I'd read it before in primary school, so I don't know why it says 'fourth years only'.

What is required is a varied programme of guided reading where, instead of ploughing an ever deepening furrow down a single track, pupils can question more fully the kinds of books available to them.

In the second part of the book I shall be describing some of the ways teachers of 10- and 11-year olds have worked to broaden their classes approach to reading beyond Roald Dahl and, without being prescriptive, allow pupils to develop frames of reference which allow them to make more informed choices in their personal reading. Prior to that, however, first I want to explore another factor at work in the response to any kind of reading and which I touched on in describing Tim and Jennie's responses, namely the gender of the reader.

Implications for the reading curriculum

1 The ability to make sense of new texts depends on children's past experience of other stories so that in the middle years of schooling children need to encounter a wide range of genre and have the opportunity to discuss them with each other as a class or group.

2 Children's unguided choice rarely provides the variety important for development.

3 Teachers need to influence their children's reading by regularly recommending new books to them and by ensuring the provision of a wide range of genre as well as levels of reading difficulty.

4 Reading needs to be seen as an important part of the curriculum and not something to fill in time when other work has been completed, or as a quiet activity at the end of the day.

5 Teachers should positively model the role of the reader alongside their children.

6 Individual reading offers limited opportunities for developing an ability to discuss and evaluate stories. Children need opportunities to read in groups and share stories for particular purposes together.

7 Children need more help in understanding what being a good reader involves. Pupils' records of their reading need to involve more than recording likes and dislikes. Teachers need to record how each child approaches new reading tasks and the strategies each uses to make sense of unfamiliar material.

3 Building communities of readers

'Independent', 'free', 'private', 'personal' are all terms used in schools to describe the time teachers give to their pupils' unguided reading. What all these attributes have in common is an emphasis on the solitary nature of the reading process and the individual involvement of the learner. They are the visible signs of a rationale behind a reading model that emphasises that children develop their reading skills by the act of reading and that the best way to ensure each individual's growth is to provide adequate time to read books which engage their interests. The solitary nature of the activity is further reinforced by classroom practices such as USSR (uninterrupted, sustained, silent reading) and prevalent images of good readers being 'bookworms' who are to be found at their desk, or in the book corner 'lost in books'. The reader is seen as egocentric, completely unaware of the external world and without responsibility to others.

The one relationship that is stressed as important in the school reading process is that of teacher to pupil. For some teachers this relationship is that of an instructor, sampling the child's oral reading in order to check on progress. Many primary school teachers consider hearing children read regularly to be one of their most important teaching roles. A further development of this one-to-one relationship exists in classrooms with an emphasis on 'real books' where the accent is on matching book to reader. This commits the teacher to familiarize herself with the pupils' current interests and personal circumstances as well as reading ability. The powerful message, that reading is an individual activity dependent on particular tastes and personal experience, remains.

Reading fiction, however, depends as much for its sustenance on communities of readers who share common interests and exchange views on the latest book they have read, as on an individual reading alone. On a personal level, this is done whenever a friend asks someone if they have read a particular book and whets the appetite for the next good read. On the public level, there is a whole body of people earning a living by selecting and reviewing new books for the 'serious' press and weekend supplements and a range of literary prizes that create new markets and interests in reading. Without this free exchange of ideas, which work to establish common viewpoints and shared practices of interpretation, books could not be brought to the attention of a public and would not be worth the printing.

In academic communities, too, studies of trends in criticism since 1970 (Eagleton, 1983: 54–90) have emphasised the importance of the shared habits of reading and the critical practices tacitly agreed by readers of literature. Jonathan Culler used the term 'communities of readers' to describe reading as an interpersonal process in which meaning is arrived at in a particular way because of learned interpretative strategies. 'Meaning is not an individual creation but the result of applying to the text operations and conventions which constitute the institution of literature' (Culler, 1981). Wolfgang Iser (1978) has argued that readers unlock the potential of literary text by applying to them the reading strategies they have learned. For Iser's reader a text itself offers a 'structure of appeal' and 'horizons of expectation' with gaps and indeterminacies that the 'implied' reader works through to create an aesthetically pleasing whole. For Stanley Fish (1980) the prior interpretative procedures are the key element in any reading response. These are the aspects of literary knowledge, assumptions and strategies that produce readings within a particular framework. Both these academics emphasize the reader's power and control over the text which comes from shared ways of reception.

At the popular level, readers' expectations of what particular authors or genres offer are of equal importance, and are always the consideration of the writer eager to sell books by creating more of the same. In children's publishing for example, Enid Blyton's phenomenal success, which resulted in one in ten children naming her as their favourite author in 1983, can be attributed in part to her concern to make direct contact with her audience. Blyton was successful in creating a sense of community through encouraging her readers to write to each other, to write to her with new ideas for adventures which she frequently used and even by organizing them to collect blankets and silver paper for good causes (Leeson, 1985: 168). By these methods she reinforced their self-identification as Blyton readers, ensuring a ready market for each new publication.

In discussing the selection of texts for 'A' level English Literature classes I have identified a 'tyranny of taste' that can be exercised in the name of good literature and which privileges certain kinds of reading (Millard, 1988: 5–19). The effect is to make readers apologetic about an interest in reading if it is not readily identifiable as having literary merit. In some circles reading popular fiction seems to be more worrying than reading no books at all. And yet popular fiction readers have an important role to play in sustaining publishing and creating an environment in which creativity can flourish. Their importance stressed by Robert Leeson (1985):

This popular readership of books not only guarantees the continued publication of the 'easy' and the 'superficial', but also guarantees the future of the Literature with a capital 'L'. Indeed it has already done so. Literature with a limited readership appeal often depends for its life on two subsidies, one from the public, whatever their tastes in books, and one from popular authors on the publisher's list.

It is essential then, when planning a reading programme, to start by acknowledging and understanding children's tastes in reading but this does not also mean accepting that these tastes should determine the books that the class, as a community, will share. Charles Sarland, in a recent book describing methods of developing narrative understanding with older secondary pupils, is willing to accept the tastes of a proportion of his class in the choice of James Herbert's *The Fog* as a basis for examination course work. He argues it is the 'narrative technique', rather than the gratuitous violence and explicit sex, that make it a suitable object for group study. His argument is based on an anti-elitist stance which argues for the importance of the reader's engagement and emotional satisfaction with what is being read unimpeded by the teacher's judgement of literary worth. In making this particular choice he prioritizes the importance of the pleasure element of their reader response to a readerly or readily consumable text. The pupil's stated interest is taken as paramount, even though an earlier survey he had conducted in school had shown that younger classes reported some titles as popular because they had been read to them by the teacher in class (Sarland, 1990). In other words he provides some contrary evidence that children's tastes can be influenced by the community of readers set up by the teacher's selection of books for a particular group. Sarland achieves his immediate teaching goal of grabbing the class's attention but there is a blindness to some of the other messages he is being given; for example, the tastes of the girl in the class who suggests 'it's just the sort of thing you get in dirty porno films, that's all'. What seems more important than identifying the particular texts which might gratify pupils' immediate interests is understanding how teachers can establish a classroom climate in which the reading and sharing of books becomes an accepted and regular part of pupils' expectations so that their range of reading is broadened and they are enabled to read with greater flexibility and with more insight.

In a study conducted in the secondary sector at the beginning of the 1980s, on a much smaller scale than that of Frank Whitehead's national survey (Whitehead *et al.*, 1974), Alastair West sought to identify and analyse the ways in which secondary schools contribute to the formation of readers. His intention was to identify the classroom practices and processes which lie behind what he describes as 'the age class and gender inflected national readership figures'. His programme of interviews conducted in three large comprehensive schools focused on the reading habits of a 162 14–16-year olds and their perceptions of fiction. The six class teachers involved were all described as having an equal commitment to the importance of fiction in the curriculum and its ability to facilitate a greater understanding of the self, the world and others. Yet 'on every measure employed', West found fiction reading was very much more successfully established in one school than in the other two. Moreover, the successful school was the one whose social composition might have suggested least likelihood of commitment to reading. The pupils in this school not only read more widely but they did so irrespective of social class, school ability group, or gender.

West concluded that the reason for the real difference in attitude to reading was that in this particular school the pupils spent between a third and a quarter of their allocated English time in reading books of their own choice in addition to studying a class text. The students perceived reading, which included choosing and talking about books, to be an important component of their learning in English, whereas pupils in the other two schools did not. A very small number of the students in the other two schools rated reading as their favourite activity whereas a large number of the successful school's pupils did.

School policy encouraged reading by granting the pupils autonomy in questions of choice and freedom of access to the library while giving reading status by making it a major focus of the school reporting system. The school created a committed community of readers in Jonathan Culler's terms by creating shared practices and encouraging informal dialogue about books. It was this aspect of reading, the effect of the school on children's understanding of the reading process and the kind of reading communities teachers were either consciously or unconsciously creating that most interested me when I set about my enquiry into the current state of children's attitudes to reading. Both Whitehead and West had demonstrated clearly that there was a marked decline in reading between the ages of 10+ and 14 in most schools. Whitehead located the reason for this in the number of activities competing for a teenager's leisure time. He appears to identify an increasing divergence of reading habits precipitated by the increase in alternative forms of narrative gratification available through cinema and television. West shows that schools, to a certain extent, can reverse this trend by being responsive to individual children's needs.

In the small sample of schools I studied there were definite norms of behaviour and expectations among the children's peer groups that either promoted or hampered their willingness to read. Schools with positive attitudes to reading not only made time for reading by setting aside daily periods, USSR (uninterrupted, sustained, silent reading) or ERIC (everyone reading in class) but also emphasized the social nature of reading by creating just as many opportunities for talking about and sharing the class's responses, asking questions about, and looking for answers in, books. On the negative side, one school which had a teacher who, when interviewed, expressed a particular commitment to personal reading also reluctantly acknowledged his own class's resistance to the notion of being a good reader. Individuals had admitted to thinking reading was important to them as a skill they needed in later life, because 'if you do get a job, then they want you to write summat down, you might not know how to spell it, if you can't read'.

However, admitting to liking school reading was a very different matter. Shairon, a pupil of the school, described as a competent reader by the teacher, hesitated when asked whom she thought read the most in her class. It was a question she had never thought of asking for herself and she was hesitant in making suggestions.

Shairon: I don't know. I don't think – people like to say . . . I don't think they really like reading very much but they can read well. Yeah, they can read well but I wouldn't say that they enjoyed reading.

Interviewer: But you do enjoy reading, don't you? And you said earlier that gets you called a swot, a teacher's pet. So, what do you think about that?

Shairon: I just ignore them. I told me mum about it and me mum says, 'Oh just ignore them, they'll soon get bored if you ignore what they're saying.'

Interviewer: Why do you think they call you names like that?

Shairon: I don't know. They call it this other girl called Vicki as well 'cos she likes reading and things like that.

When she was asked if there was anyone in her class who had interesting things to say about books and who she could discuss books with, her answer was an emphatic no. The antagonistic peer group attitudes to those who enjoyed reading were corroborated by one of the boys in the class who suggested that reading was something he and his friends would always 'keep quiet about'. When asked to say more about why his friends did not discuss books he said:

'I don't know. I think if they just tell everyone people will probably just leave them alone and think they're a swot. They just keep on and on at you and just call you a 'swot, swot, swot', like that, and just get round you and keep calling it you and so you end up having a fight and then you get done for having a fight.'

He went on to explain that he knew reading was important in the real world and necessary to get a good job but he was equally aware being caught with your head in a book in his class means being ostracized from the social group. Given the chance to discuss things together there are more important issues than the contents of a book claiming his friends' attention:

'Mostly on my table all they ever talk about is computer games. Sometimes you, like, they bring, like, these instruction books to school and they read them. They talk about their reading, but only computer reading. You're not allowed them any more now. You're only allowed story books.'

In banning the magazines that this group enjoyed discussing the teacher's intentions were good. He expected the class to read more demanding materials but by banning the computer magazines from what he presented as voluntary reading time he not only showed that the free choice on offer is illusory but he also lost a source of reading that could motivate the group. Perhaps one of the problems for pupils in this class is that they have been taught to associate reading with getting jobs, but the kind of reading they are asked to in private reading time does not match any of these expectations. When he described the school's policy on reading, the teacher was clearly ambivalent about the benefits to be gained from the provision of a fixed reading period:

'Institutionalized in this school is a silent reading period every day, and that's been in place at least two years now. So these children are very used to that period of silent reading, twenty minutes, after lunch. I get a feeling sometimes that it's resented, that they actually don't want to. So rather than there be a period, or one or two periods, during school timetable when I choose when there is a silent period, when we all read together, it's institutionalized, it's a kind of settling down thing. I feel to some extent that it's spoilt some of the magic that might be involved in the reading process because it's been so institutionalized like that. And their attitude to reading in that sense is not a very good one. They don't like it.'

What he described is a school policy that he felt discouraged a commitment to reading rather than promoted it. Books were used to 'settle children down' after lunch instead of being located in an active part of the day when they could concentrate well. He suggested that the rather negative attitude to personal reading expressed by the three pupils interviewed was widespread in the school and that the children have arrived in his class with an antagonistic attitude to reading time. In describing this attitude he also associated the word 'swot' with the committed reader:

'Well I think it's probably one of the things where reading is like being a swot and it's certainly not cool to be a swot and even the best reader will sit there with her book open, but not be reading the book, be more interested in chewing gum, or trying to have a little chat. They will take a long time to settle down. Having said that, one of the things some of them actually enjoy is going – and again this is a positive feature, very positive feature really – is going and helping the younger classes with reading so they are actually sitting down and helping them with books. But actually, as to picking up a book, seems that bit of a chore sometimes, you know, that you've actually got to get through it. Some of them say, "I've read this book, I don't like it, can I change it?" and that will happen quite often.'

One of the teacher's methods for improving the children's reading was based on a textbook, *Scope for Reading*, which contained reading passages followed by what the teacher described as

'searching questions which are not obvious. The answers to them are not necessarily right and wrong answers, there's open answers to the questions and so usually I would read the passage with the children, have children read the passage out, discuss it with them.'

He also described the class's irritation at having to look at questions in detail but suggested that the practice was important:

'because I think they do lack confidence when it comes to having a kind of deeper understanding of the material that they're presented with which I think that helps me provide.'

Comprehension of what has been read and the need to find information for a particular purpose has therefore been bracketed off from the choosing of books and reading for pleasure. Yet wide reading is something he valued for his class and in discussing its place in the National Curriculum he commented:

'I mean, really for me it's the beginning of thinking about it; I really feel as though I want to try and get children interested in books and books for their own sake and the pleasure of books.'

However there was also an accompanying feeling that it is now too late for these particular children:

'When I've got to this stage, most of the children know the mechanics of reading, but this class is not interested in reading. That's what I've been given. And so, at 12 years old, 11 to 12 years old, these children are not interested in reading. Now I haven't examined how they've been taught, but they all know how to read.'

There is a tacit acceptance of the pupils' lack of enthusiasm for reading as a given that cannot be changed and which is separate from the teacher's responsibility for giving practice in 'the mechanics' of reading for which he believed had made good provision.

Indeed, within the class the peer pressure not to read was a particularly strong one because the girls were as diffident about claiming the title 'good reader' as the boys and felt uneasy about admitting their interest in books. This was unusual, for girls in the other primary schools had all described supportive networks of readers within their friendship groups and often commented that it was girls who enjoyed reading and swapping their books whilst it was boys who were seen to be less enthusiastic and lacking in concentration in class. Ambivalence about the place of private reading in the curriculum, however, was a feature of all but one of the primary schools in the survey. One teacher went so far as to say that with all the pressures of the National Curriculum, reading fiction with the children seemed like a luxury in which she could not always afford to indulge.

Many teachers seemed less certain of their role as teachers of reading once children had learned what were seen as the basics skills. There was little sense of reading as a continuous learning process which depended on providing pupils with an opportunity to meet complex texts and on helping them to read them appropriately. There was also very little sense of children's reading abilities being perceived as existing on a variety of levels with the accompanying need to make provision for both able and weaker readers. This uncertainty about the teacher's role in developing more advanced reading skills was most evident in the tacit messages given by the times in school allotted for reading and the expectations created by the choices. If the school whose pupils were reluctant to read implied that reading was for 'settling down', other schools used reading as a filling-in space where other activities could be completed, especially by the teachers. One teacher from a middle school, located in an area of expensive housing and well-educated families, again began the interview by emphasizing the importance of reading, measured both by the provision of books by special times set aside for it:

> 'They have a whole load of fiction books that are in the year base that they can choose as they want and then we have two sessions in the week which are specified for silent reading when they have to read.'

But she quickly modified her initial statement, adding:

> 'unless they play the recorder and that's when the recorder sessions go on.'

In fact, a large number of the children were involved in recorders so that for them the message was that reading is optional and those left to read saw it as a time filler with no particular curriculum importance.

The timing of the reading sessions was also significant; they were held last thing on Tuesdays and Thursdays. Positioning reading at the end of the day, in the way that story time is often used in the infant school, suggests it is a closing-down activity that demands less concentration and which many children will see as a preparation for going home. It was often used by the staff as a substitute for non-contact time. Many finished off their marking or tidied their classrooms. Her feeling came over strongly that the children in her school had already developed as good readers so there was less of a role for teacher to play.

> 'I think we're very fortunate in having children here who get such a lot of backing from home. I would imagine a lot of them can read very well before they even get to this school because of the help they've had from home.'

Another important contribution to reading development was made by access to public library resources:

> 'Our children also use the local library a lot; so much so that we had a phone call last week to ask, "Please would you tell us when you're doing a topic so we can get a few more books in, because we've been inundated by requests." . . . Often we'll have a stack of great thick books brought in about a particular topic without even having to ask. They just appear, so they know at home where to go and look for things.'

In terms of school provision, both of time and resources, the focus on reading seems very marginal, as if it were not the role of the teacher to help children with the choice of fiction or to monitor the reading levels and reliability of the information books brought in. The hidden message given by the school, that reading is an individual's own responsibility, was confirmed by her final remarks:

'Reading is very much an incidental part of their work because it's like adults –
you read because you know how to read and you want to find the information
rather than because you've got to read.'

Such an attitude can help pupils to be independent in their learning where
they are well motivated, but it can also encourage the avoidance techniques of
the following pupil, a girl who chooses to read only *Sweet Valley High* books
and finds the fiction in the school library 'boring'. She explains she likes to
spend her time in the library browsing through the books without committing
herself to reading:

'I haven't really read many, I just pick them up, read the back and then if I have
to go and sit down again, I'll pick that book and just read any page . . .'

Not only this, but even where children make positive choices these may be
very limited in the range of cultural experiences they offer.

Reflecting other cultures

One of the major problems of leaving much of the choice of books to the
individual and outside sources, such as public libraries, generous relatives and
W.H. Smiths, is that whole areas of reading experience can be neglected. A
frequent casualty of poor book-selection policies is the provision of a range of
stories which reflect cultures other than white Anglo-Saxon Britons and
Americans. If one of the aims of wide-ranging reading is to enable pupils to see
the world through others' eyes and to get different perspectives on both the
past and the present, then more active book-selection policies are needed. Any
rapid survey of the children's section of a large bookshop reveals how sparse
representations of black and Asian cultures are in the books suitable for the
middle-age range. Perhaps this relative scarcity in the commercial market
explains the limitations of the book recommendation in the April 1993 rewrite
of the English Orders. Under a sub-heading 'Texts drawn from a variety of
cultures and traditions' only three titles appear, one of which, Anita Desai's
The Village by the Sea, had previously been read in schools by children a good
deal older than eleven. Although the National Currriculum's proposals are
intended to ensure that pupils read widely and are introduced to other cultural
traditions, as well as writers 'of central importance to the literary tradition', it
is these latter that are given prominence in Key Stage Two.

Gunther Kress, writing in the *Times Educational Supplement* of the need for
an English curriculum that meets the needs of the twenty-first century, places
a high priority on the role of English in developing a thorough understanding
of the values and meanings of contemporary society. He suggests (TES Plat-
form, 12 February 1993)

. . . these can be explored through the study of salient texts of all the society's
cultural groups. Knowledge of a wide variety of texts from the mundane to the

aesthetically valued, provides an understanding that there are many ways of being in the world and of seeing the world.

The limited number of children from other cultural backgrounds whom I interviewed about their personal preference, described difficulty in finding books that reflected their own cultures. Anne-Marie, whose family came from Jamaica, suggested that there were very few books in the school library that had people from her community. She said:

> 'They have them [books about black people] in the library in town but they don't bring them to our school. I have chosen quite a few but some of the ones that are about people like me have, like, long words.'

Even less in evidence at this stage were a range of books in any language other than English, despite the presence of children for whom English was their second language. There is often a mistaken belief that bilingual children should only practise reading in English because there is a general tendency to define literacy as an ability to read and write English. Research, however, shows there are many benefits from the ability to read fluently in the first language that can be used in the development of the second. Evidence from the former ILEA Research and Statistics branch showed that 'fully fluent bilingual pupils were the most experienced readers of all' (quoted in Barrs and Thomas, 1991: 92).

Aware that biliteracy produces flexible readers who can draw on a range of linguistic knowledge the Cox Report (DES, 1988) recommended that:

> Work should start from the pupil's own linguistic competence. Many pupils are bilingual and sometimes biliterate, and quite often literally know more about language than their teachers, at least in some respects.

It is also possible to provide a range of books where the language difference is a question of alternative versions of English, such as Faustin Charles, *The Kiskadee Queen*, a collection of African and Afro-American nursery rhymes and song, or John Agard's Caribbean proverbs and poems, *Say It Again Granny*. Such collections help children value their home experience of creative language play and story telling, and also allow all children to share stories from cultures different from their own. However, there was very little evidence that the need to provide books from a range of cultures had been adequately addressed in any of the schools in which I conducted interviews.

Reading communities in the first years of secondary school

The reading habits that I found established in the last stages of primary school were also mirrored in the secondary phase of schooling, determining how the pupils see themselves as readers and whose recommendations they are likely to follow. For many children the main influence on whether they are interested readers is determined by their home circumstances and their families' interests. A clear example of this is provided by Christine, a 12-year old in her first year of secondary education, who explained most clearly how she shared her books with both her friends and her family. Interestingly, it is her mother who has bought books for her in the past; books she describes as 'old classic books' and now her mother 'likes reading books that I read . . . If I say a books really interesting, then she'll read it as well.' She also valued the opinions of her friends and used a library outside school where she and her friend exchanged views on the books they borrow:

> 'Yeah, I do go to the library with my friend, not this school library and I sometimes say, "Can I have a look at your book?" and then she'll tell me if it's a good book or not. If she found it boring then I wouldn't read it.'

She is also aware of the books other members of her family are reading:

> 'My sister's done a project about the relationship between a mother and her children, and she has a book where it has the letters that are from mothers to their children and from the children to their mothers and from these you can tell the kind of relationships they had with each other. If it was a very polite letter you could tell that it wasn't a very close relationship. But some girls would tell things like, "Oh, I fell out with my friend at school" and if they can tell their mother that, then you can tell they have a close relationship. So I like that book. That's the book that my sister is reading . . .
>
> My brother had the autobiography of Malcolm X and I read that as well. I don't agree with everything he wrote but there's something, he had a way of saying things that he really, you know, you thought about deeply . . . other people, when they say things, you think about it for a while and then you forget.'

The book that Christine is currently reading independently in class, at the time of the interview, has also come from a member of her family. It is *The Godfather*, not a book that teachers would recommend for private reading in Y7. Christine, however, was not embarrassed to talk about this book. She explained it was an 'old book' she has read many times; 'its a brilliant book so I read it again and again'.

The communities of readers that Christine chooses to belong to have been formed, for the most part, outside of school. Her choice of private reading seems rather directionless and the school or her teacher have had very little influence on her choice. This is exactly the state of affairs described by the primary school teacher who relied on parents and libraries to provide suitable reading for the class rather than forming her own picture of each individual's reading and helping their individual choice. I was left speculating about those children whose parents did not provide them with books, introduce them to libraries or motivate their reading. What attitudes would they bring with them to the secondary phase of education?

In the secondary school curriculum, however, there was another community available to help shape Christine's response to reading, provided by her English class. She described class work on Penelope Lively's *The Ghost of Thomas Kempe* which she had read two years earlier but which her teacher had made more interesting:

> 'He was talking about alchemy and those old-fashioned words and that there were certain clues that we knew that had been written a long time ago, and before we wouldn't have known that alchemy and all these words and now we've got a good idea of what these words mean, even though they were written a long time ago, but before we wouldn't have taken an interest in them.'

Closer reading of the text and an engagement with the story through writing has helped Christine understand more than when she had read the book herself. The kind of focus provided by joint creative work on a book shared in class is not a substitute for wide and independent reading but it does ensure a shared experience of story and allows pupils to build up strategies for discussing what they read. Unfortunately, the provision of multiple copies of class readers is rare in the last years of the primary school, so that many children miss out on a stage of group reading and sharing opinions on a story directed by the teacher. The emphasis on children's voluntary reading has the effect of marginalizing fiction to reading practice or centring its importance on project work.

One deputy head teacher with a special interest in language work described how she liked to use small sets of books in groups so that the children could deal with something appropriate to their interests and abilities and also have someone with whom to discuss their reading. She also reluctantly admitted that she had not found an opportunity to do this recently: 'we read literature to the children, although I do find that the National Curriculum is edging that out a little bit; time is so precious'.

As in Alastair West's study, I also discovered one school in my survey where habits of reading in the junior phase were better established. The attitudes of both pupils and teachers stood out in marked contrast to the other primary schools where I had conducted interviews. Here an interest in reading seemed equally established in boys and girls who accepted it as part both of their everyday conversations and school work. There remained differences of interest between the genders which I will explore in Chapter 5, but there were far more points of agreement among boys and girls in the class than in any other. The school itself was situated on the edge of the city and drew its children from a large council estate with a small private estate of newer modestly priced housing. Many children had supportive parents but there was not the same contribution to the reading matter from home or the same support in terms of specialist knowledge.

In Chapter 2 I described Shairon's surprise when she was asked who had interesting things to say about books in her class. She had also been unable to name the kinds of books her friends enjoyed. In contrast, Helen, who also began by naming Enid Blyton as her favourite writer, described sharing many more writers with the other members of her social group. She knew exactly what the other girls in her class were reading and discussed their willingness to help with selection of new stories:

> 'My friends talk about books and say more about them, what they've read, they would recommend them to you. Sometimes you pick up a book and say, "Have you read this?", and if they say, "No," then you have to like try it or something. If they say "No, it's not very good," then I won't read it.'

She was unsure, however, of the kinds of books that the boys read but Jamie, from the same class, who was a slower reader, immediately named another boy as someone who had interesting things to say about books. Jamie explained that he could tell his friend was interested in books because:

> 'When he writes them down in his comment book he's always going mad because he thinks they're mega and that lot and good. And he always says . . . "Daryl, I didn't know this," and I'm gonna get this again.'

Jamie says he takes a lot of notice of what his friend has to say about reading and when he was asked directly if there was anyone in the class who disliked reading he stated emphatically that no-one disliked reading.

Matthew, from the same class, described by his teacher as an average reader, stated a preference for poetry rather than fiction. He had followed up the recommendations of his teacher and those of a poet who had been invited to talk to the class. He was also able to explain how a friend helped him sort out some difficult information about golf technique in a reference book.

Matthew: I was having difficulty deciding about something, but I asked my friend to read it and then he told me what he thought about it.
Interviewer: And what did it say that you weren't sure about?
Matthew: It was just these brackets that kept turning it around and I didn't know. I wasn't sure what it was. I was really stuck so I just asked Gareth and then he read from a certain part where I was stuck at and he says, 'Oh it's simple, it's just telling you what it makes.' And then he just explained it to me; so he's probably a better reader than me, or he understands it.

Matthew's ability to consult a friend about reading, to take his advice and acknowledge his superior skill at making sense of the information is the result of the atmosphere of collaborative enterprise and mutual support surrounding reading tasks in this class. All three pupils, despite their varied levels of ability, had positive things to say about themselves and their peer group as readers, so perhaps it was not so surprising to find the same commitment in the teacher. It is sometimes thought that the teachers who offer the best model to this age group of reading are those who have made language their speciality. Surprisingly, the teacher concerned was more interested in the Science and Technology curriculum and, as the consultant for the school, was particularly skilled in the teaching of computers. However, his commitment to the class's reading was equally evident and had as its foundation a commitment to selecting books that were appropriate and which widened pupils' access to information.

'In addition to the books which we have in school anyway, which are reading books bought in the normal way, over the past number of years we've participated in the library bus lending scheme when the big library van comes to school and we let children actually go on the bus and choose, literally, hundreds of books which we retain for the whole of that year. And that's usually a very strong extra resource. We do it on a class basis, with something like 30 or 40 books per class, which each age group regularly changes round, so the children in the course of a year might have access to something like 150 extra quality reading books that they wouldn't normally have.'

This emphasis on the selection of books is part of a whole school philosophy about the importance of what the teacher calls 'quality books that stand on their own, and that are not related to any kind of reading scheme.' He suggested that a key issue in the school's policy was the continuing involvement of parents in a shared reading scheme to encourage reading at home.

'We've tried to educate the parents as well into using these new books to make them realise that they are a better substitute than reading schemes, because obviously many parents believe, who were taught in that way, that schemes are the way to do it, and understand, see progression through reading, as a step from going through A to B. The best way we've found of getting this over has been to involve them completely in the way that their children choose their books and getting them involved in making comments about them.'

He explained also that this commentary on the reading by the parents is maintained throughout the school, so that the comment book acted as a kind of diary in which the parent or the teacher is free to record whatever they like. As the children get older they took charge of the record themselves, writing little reviews about the book or making their own personal comments about a particular book. He explained that flexibility is needed to provide for all the children's needs. Slower readers still have access to good picture stories but he also involved the whole class in producing stories for particular pupils with special needs.

'What I've done quite a lot is actually get other children to produce reading materials for some of the less able children. So, because I've been into sort of desk-top publishing as well and using the sort of new facilities that are available to us with the new range of computers that have come out, the children work in pairs to produce stories. On one occasion they were all called "Craig Stories", devised to help a boy of this name with his reading. The children used him as a central character and wrote amusing little stories about him and various adventures that he had. They wrote all these up on the computer and saved them as files which were then loaded into the desk-top publishing package and produced as quality type books with really nice typeface which the children then illustrated and turned them into a series of "Craig Stories", which was really killing quite a lot of birds with one stone. First of all we were producing material for him that he was going to be heavily involved with, as well as producing just amusing stories for themselves to read.'

Through these strategies, the reading needs of individual children were met in a variety of ways, from continuing adult support for those who needed it, to a combined class effort to provide interesting stories for the slower readers. The pupils' responses in the interviews bore out their teacher's claim for the centrality of reading in their learning experience. They were eager to talk about their books, recalling both those they had read together and the books they had recorded in their diaries.

At the time of the interviews, the whole class were occupied with a story writing project and were reading a range of books in order to find out what made a good story in a particular genre. They were considering the different appeals of mystery stories, and fairy tales and were using their personal reading tastes to get ideas for their own collection of short stories which they were working on in small groups. This was later published and sold to parents and governors as *Seven Stories by Class Seven*. (An excerpt from one of these stories called, *Jack strikes it Lucky*, is reproduced in Chapter 4.)

At the heart of the reading curriculum in this school was a provision for time spent on choosing and discussing their choice as well as the provision reading time. When the teacher began to describe the organization of the reading sessions there did not appear to be much difference between the 'institutionalized' reading periods of the school with reluctant readers or the time set aside by some teachers for getting on with their own routine tasks. He described his strategy for establishing reading in similar terms to other teachers interviewed in the survey:

'Well what I try, partly for my own sanity than anything else, is every morning, the very first thing that they do is to go to get some kind of reading material. I mean, initially it's always a story-book, but as the year progresses that reading material often spills over into their own interests, where they will sit and read quietly for at least ten or fifteen minutes, because, as I say to them, "If you manage to do that every morning, first thing, five times 15 minutes, you've actually read for at least an hour and a quarter that week. And it works, well at least I've found it works because it becomes a habit with them. They come in, they settle down, they get on with some kind of reading. I know that this guarantees they are going to have a minimum of an hour and a half reading a week, plus anything else that they either do voluntarily or in their own time or which I set up later in the week. It's just a really agreeable, quiet way to start the day. I take the register and they're free to change their book in the sort of the five minutes lull after that. And then, depending on what's on, or what I've got to do, I'll let that reading period extend until I feel that it's coming to a sort of natural end or we need to get on with something else. On Friday morning I use that as an extended reading period where I chase up all the kids who may need extra attention and check that most people have kept their records up-to-date.'

What made the difference in this class was the teacher's own commitment to following up their individual reading, making sure that children's choices matched their ability as well as their interests. The range of ability in this class differed very little from that in the class whose teacher described his pupils as having 'mastered the basics of reading'. However, this teacher was far more aware of the range of skills in the group and could identify readily those who required more practice and encouragement to become independent in their reading habits.

My sample of classrooms is a small one, but my overall findings, that it is not the initial teaching of reading that creates difficulties for teachers, but finding adequate time for the promotion of wider reading and strategies that nourish children's continuing interest, correspond closely to reports from the HMI. Following a survey of primary schools to examine the *Implementation of the Curricular Requirements of ERA in its First Year* (1989–90) they stated:

> In those [schools] which were most successful, pupils often heard well chosen stories which they explored through shared enjoyment and discussion

but added

> Often teachers were uncertain about how to promote enthusiasm for reading – much remains to be done to ensure the widespread and effective development of reading beyond the initial stages, to develop the habit of voluntary reading.

This, in its turn, is a reiteration of the findings of the Bullock Committee (DES, 1975) when they found:

> The teaching of reading virtually ceases once the child can read with reasonable accuracy at reasonable speed. Yet to discontinue instruction at this point is rather like halting the training of a pianist once he can play the scales and a few elementary tunes.

If by 'teaching reading' we intend to indicate some continuing interaction between pupil and teacher who has carefully thought out strategies for dealing with different kinds of reading materials, then my study of reading in the last years of the primary school largely reflects the same state of affairs. There is little common understanding of the kind of reading which children are expected to undertake once the teachers believe they are reading independently, or as to what class approaches to structured close reading of stories and information are appropriate.

In recording individual's reading, most teachers are happy with a simple comment book where the child records the title of her current reading book, sometimes the page reached and an indication of whether the book was enjoyed. Often this is recorded with the ubiquitous smiling face or star system without a comment at all. The simple record system owes something to the remnants of reading schemes where recording the book, its level and page gave some indication of progress in graded reading. In free reading it allows the teacher to monitor the kind of books being read, but is unable to give any indication of the level of response or the pupil's ability to pick out significant details for comment. In practice, many children are allowed to drop the habit of recording during the later years. A more expansive model for written records would be the kinds of structured interview and detailed records advocated by the *Primary Language Record* (Barrs *et al.* 1988) produced by the Centre for Language in Primary Education. This involves collating information on a child's reading development from a variety of sources using both a matrix to relate reading to social contexts and a planned interview system. It enables the teacher to keep track of the context of children's reading, the variety of reading materials and parents' and children's assessments of progress and difficulties.

Teachers of junior children who have been shown this detailed interview structure are alarmed at the amount of time it would take at a period when the curriculum is becoming more and more crowded with subject content. However, if the records are gradually accumulated over a period of time, rather than as a major assessment at the end of a year, or key stage in education, the task appears less daunting. The compilers of *The Reading Book* state 'Most of what we have come to know about children learning to read in recent years, is a direct result of what Yetta Goodman has termed "kid-watching" record keeping based on observation' (Barrs and Thomas, 1991) and show that reading diaries, structured interviews and reading conferences give a far more detailed insight into the way children become more and more sophisticated in their response to books.

Unfortunately, whenever the question of reading is raised as part of a political agenda there it is accompanied by pressure for the adoption of a sure fire method of instruction that will instantly raise standards. The Bullock Committee described the way they were pressurized in 1975 and it is worthwhile reminding ourselves of the way they responded:

> There was an expectation that we would identify the one method in whose adoption lay the whole solution. Let us therefore express our conclusion at the outset in plain terms: there is no one method, medium, approach, device or philosophy that holds the key to the process of learning to read. We believe that the knowledge does exist to improve the teaching of reading but that it does not lie in the triumphant discovery, or re-discovery, of a particular formula. Simple endorsements of one or another nostrum are no service to the teaching of reading. A glance at the past reveals the truth of this. The main arguments of how reading should be taught have been repeated over and over again as the decades pass, but the problems remain.

In September 1992, only three years after the introduction of the National Curriculum in English and before the cohorts of 11- and 14-year-old children had been tested, the Secretary of State chose to announce what the press described as 'far-reaching changes' in the teaching of English. These changes have the effect of suggesting that certain methods of teaching reading, certain kinds of reading material should take priority over others. As reported by

Colin Hughes (Education Editor, *The Independent*, 10 September 1992) the proposals were that:

> Primary teachers be required by law to use phonics and reading schemes along-
> side other methods with infants who are learning to read. It would in effect
> become illegal to rely exclusively on 'real books' and 'look and say' methods. The
> council will also prescribe a list of set works or authors to which all school pupils
> should be introduced.

More outrageously,

> Hit Squads Target Trendy Teachers

was the report by Patrick Hennessy (Education Correspondent, *Daily Express* the same day). Once more, as in 1975, the panacea of an imposed method of reading instruction in the early years, is being sought although the whole of the evidence from schools and HMI reports points to the simple fact that there are no short cuts to developing reading experience.

Subsequent enquiries have found that most teachers in the early years spend a good deal of reading time in direct instruction. The Warwick University Evaluation of the National Curriculum Core subjects, commissioned by the Government, recorded in its interim report, published in August 1992, that in their classroom observations they found that in the first three years of school:

> The teaching of phonics occurs for a quarter of the total time devoted to teach-
> ing reading. All teaching reading activities were observed to be planned and
> structured by the teacher.

Further:

> On the basis of these observations of teaching reading, we find that 54% of
> instances were concerned with teachers' teaching strategies for reading, while
> 46% were focused on reading as an activity in itself . . . When the time spent is
> analysed in a similar way, teachers are seen to spend more time (60%) on
> teaching strategies for reading than providing for reading itself (40%).

The report found less evidence of direct teaching of what are described as 'higher order reading skills' in the middle phase, finding evidence in only 3 out of 33 classroom sessions observed. Dictionary use accounted for nearly half of the observed instances of advanced reading skills with exercise on alphabetical order, finding synonyms, checking spelling of a word and looking up the meaning of a word making up the rest. Teachers also stated in their interviews that the National Curriculum had not influenced their choice of reading texts.

Leaving aside the question of whether 'direct teaching' is the most effective way of developing reading with older juniors, the report supports my own evidence that there is far less consensus of how reading might be developed in the middle years. Teachers of secondary pupils, on the other hand, had already begun to change their choice of literature to include more pre-twentieth century material in their reading lessons (Warwick University, 1992: 7).

If children are to value reading and become more sophisticated in their personal reading habits, it is not enough to legislate for all 14-year olds to be tested on their understanding of a piece of Shakespeare and an anthology made up of orts and fragments of other works from a 'recognized canon' of great authors. Indeed, the experience of many educated adults suggests that the imposition of set books is more likely to create non-readers than vice versa. It will be even more damaging to impose a method of learning in the early years which subordinates the meaning of the text to its method of instruction and then prescribes the kind of reading that older children must experience.

What is needed for an effective reading policy is the allocation of sufficient time for reading in the curriculum and sufficient funding to ensure the full range of suitable books to be shared and used in class, including multiple copies of narrative texts for older juniors. If this choice is to succeed both in engaging children's interest and challenging their understanding it can no more be left to a simple set list of 'great works' than it can to the marketplace's offering of 'yet another up-date of Enid Blyton', or to what children recommend to each other on the grapevine. The ethos of the classroom needs to be one where the sharing of readings and the discussion of new books is as important as other attainment targets, not something that is used as a time filler or an activity that is convenient only when a written task has been completed.

There exists a well-publicized, supportive network of organizations interested in children and books which offers support to teachers in making reading a valued part of school life for everybody. This includes The School Bookshop Association, School Library Association, The Book Trust and the Educational Publishers Council, all of whom offer advice and support for book weeks, visiting writers, bookshops and book fairs. They provide expertise and sound advice, but the activities recommended such as book weeks and authors in schools involved require substantial amounts of planning and administration time as well as a commitment to expenditure. Working with children's books is not an area of the curriculum that can be sorted out once and for all in a school and then left to itself for a period of time, because collections need frequent up-dating and renewal if they are to continue to be attractive to young readers.

Teachers are influential in creating an environment where reading becomes a vital part of the learning in the classroom, but this is through shared interest, provision of time and attention not only to children's developing interests, but also to the kinds of challenges we may wish to make to their understanding of what they are reading. This implies that there are also important issues to address about the choices teachers make about presenting fiction as part of a whole language curriculum. These are the concerns I wish to address in Chapter 6, when I shall consider how teachers can help children to become more sophisticated in their response to story. Prior to that I want to consider the choices that individual pupils' make in their personal reading and how this might effect other aspects of their language learning.

Implications for the reading curriculum

1 Evidence from research, HMI, classroom observation and teacher interviews all point to the fact that there is too little time spent on actual reading tasks in the middle years of schooling. Reading needs specific timetabling and cannot be left to chance encounters or individual choice.
2 Independent reading has been made to serve too many functions in developing children's reading. There is need for more structured group activities based on a wide variety of reading tasks.
3 Experience of reading non-fiction is essential for all pupils and they need to be given help in accessing appropriate materials for specific reading purposes.
4 Schools can make a very significant difference to the attitudes children bring to their reading. The classroom is a powerful learning community and teachers who prioritize reading succeed in creating more positive attitudes and shared practices.
5 Teachers need to keep up to date with new children's fiction and update their class collections frequently.
6 Reading needs to be given a high priority within the school and pupils should have wide opportunities for exchanging books and expressing their personal opinions about what is being read.
7 All children need access to libraries which welcome their presence and where they can browse and discuss books with their peers as well as being advised by teachers, librarians and other well-informed adults.
8 Teachers should ensure that the sources of children's reading include adequate provision of books that reflect a pluralistic view of society rather than a monocultural one. Bilingual children should also have access to books in their first language to develop their understanding of genre.
9 Parents remain an important influence on their children's reading and should be involved in the development of reading beyond the early stages of learning to de-code. School bookshops, book weeks and the keeping of individual records of reading can all involve parents in the reading process.

4 Readers into writers

'Hugh Pascall was interested in time machines and he liked doing mechanical things and one day Hugh built a machine and his mum said lunch is on the table only it was too late. Off he went in his machine, back to when dinosaurs were around and there was a tunnel and Hugh was at one end and the dinosaur at the other end and Hugh said come and get me and the dinosaur went through and he got stuck and when Hugh got back his dinner was still hot.'

Hugh Pascall, age 7

Hugh was an upper infant when he wrote this story as a response to having read *Alistair's Time Machine* by Marilyn Sadler. What is most interesting about his writing is the way in which he draws on the knowledge of another story, Maurice Sendak's *Where the Wild Things Are* (1970) to provide a suitable ending. He has also learned to write a story in the third person, as a narrator, presenting himself from the outside, as the hero of the action. These are writing lessons which Hugh could only have learned from reading books and hearing books read to him.

Evidence of the influence that reading has on other aspects of language development is provided by the stories children write. This is shown not only by the kinds of subjects they choose for these stories but also by the genres they mimic and the styles of dialogue and description which they adopt. The sources of influences are not always quite as clearly signalled as those in Hugh's story but sensitivity to the resonances in children's writing and an understanding of their preferred narrative forms, can help teachers form a picture of the reading that they undertake, as well as their writing abilities. In researching children's reading interests I also collected examples of the stories they were writing to test out the hypothesis that writing was very closely linked to reading experience.

Four classes of secondary children from three very different comprehensive schools also agreed to compose personal stories of their reading development for my study. I provided their teachers with guidelines which were set out on a single side of A4.

Write the story of how you learned to read in the last school. It will help your teacher find out about the kinds of books you enjoy reading and the sort of reading you did there. Here are some of the things you could include. Write about as many of them as you like.

i. Learning to read. Who taught you? Did you find it easy or hard? Can you remember any of your first books?

ii. Reading at your last school. Things you liked reading and things you didn't enjoy. Books teachers read to you.

iii. Favourite books you've read more than once.
What are they about? Why do you like them?
Do you share books with anyone else?

iv. Do you buy any comics or magazines? Which ones?
Write about your favourite characters or features.

v. Do you like reading information books?
What do you read about in particular?

vi. Where and when do you enjoy reading?
Do you like reading to other people or reading out loud?

vii. Where do you get your books and how do you choose them?

viii. What do other people say about your reading?
(parents, teachers, friends)

The classes read the prepared list with their teachers and made suggestions about ways they might make their individual stories of reading more interesting for an outside reader. On their own initiative, one class chose to present their work in the style of one of their favourite books, magazines or comics. They described a wide range of reading interests as well as those we know to be popular, like Roald Dahl and Judy Blume. These ranged from books considered classic texts like *Huckleberry Finn* to popular adult fiction such as the horror stories of Stephen King as well as a wide selection of comics and magazines that reflected a variety of hobbies.

What was even more interesting than the titles of the books they recorded in their reading logs was the variety of formats and genre they introduced into the task. By drawing on their knowledge of comics and adventure books in structuring their accounts they revealed far more about their reading interests than are usually accounted for in their reading logs. This is particularly true of the writing of one of the keenest boys who chose to present his account in the shape of a newspaper article, although his prose style remains closer to that of personal recount (Figure 4.1).

Favourite Books
I read quite a lot of books, and I have my list of favourites like Mark Twain's *Tom Sawyer* and *Huckleberry Finn*, their life stories, Enid Blyton's *Famous Five* and *Secret Seven* series, The Hobbit, C.S. Lewis's *Tales of Narnia* and the *Depford Mice* series. I like them because they are written by good authors and they are exciting. I share them with most of my friends, and sometimes with my friends, brothers or sisters.

Comics and Magazines
It's not only books I read. I like reading magazines and comics. I like to read the computer magazine *SEGA Power* and the car magazine, *Your Car*. I also read the *Dennis the Menace* comic. My favourite articles are, in the computer magazine, the rating page and in the car magazine, the pre-season review.

The interests recorded here are wide ranging, from demanding pieces of imaginative literature to adult interest magazines. Like the young fluent readers, Margaret M. Clark (1976) found in her study, he enjoys reading non-fiction as much as stories. Two more boys presented their accounts in the style of fantasy adventure books, because these were their favourite reading material (Figure 4.2).

They both set out their writing using the strategy of asking the reader to choose from one or two optional follow-on pages in the manner of these publications. Comics also feature as a preferred model for some children's writing as in these examples (Figures 4.3 and 4.4). These accounts highlight the importance that experience of the printed word has on shaping pupils' response in a deliberate way. Pupils do not have to be consciously mimicking a particular format to show in their writing a dependence on the experience of narrative derived from their varied experience of the printed word or knowledge

The way I lernt to read

How I lernt to read.

I am able to read today thanks to three or four people who have through my life taught me to read.
I have been taught at school by teachers and at home by my mum and dad, and gradualy my reading has got better and better.
Sometimes it was easy but sometimes it was very hard. Like a lot of people my first reading books where the link-up books, picture books, Mr. Men, fairy stories and my very favorite books, one's with tapes.

Reading at my last school.

We did a lot of reading at my last school, most of it straight after we came in from lunch break. I usually read fictional books, some of them I liked so much I read them 2 or 3 times. Here are some of my favorites that I read at school). The Religious War and Enid Blyton's Famous Five series. I found most of them quiet enjoying, some weren't quiet as good but I don't thunk I disliked any at all. The teacher read a lot of books to us like Carries War,

The Dairy of Ann Frank and the Bell Tower

Favorite Books

I read quite a lot of books, and I have my list of favorites like, Mark Twain's Tom Sayer and Huckleberryfin, their life storys, Enid Blyton's Famous Five and Secret Seaven series, Hobbit, C S Lewis's Tales of Narnia and the Deptford mice series. I like them because they are written by good authors and they are exciting. I share them with most of my friends and sometimes with my friends brothers or sisters.

Comics and magazines.

It's not only books I read, I like reading magazines and comics. I like to read the computer magazine SEGA Power and the car magazine Your Car, I also read the Dennis the Menace comic. My favorite articles are, in the computer magazine the rating page, are in the car magazine the pre-search review.

The times and places I read.

I read in the car when we are traveling a long way or going on holiday.

Figure 4.1 A story of reading in the form of a newspaper of narratives in other media. Often it is important in reading children's writing to reconstruct what they have understood of a particular genre in order to unravel their intentions as writers.

In analysing the following stories I looked for the key elements of story writing identified in the original English National Curriculum document which required pupils to: 'write stories which have an opening, a setting, characters, a series of events and a resolution' (DES, 1989). In considering the series of events in each story, I have looked for the complication of plot where a narrative train is set in motion by the creation of a complication, a problem to be solved or a conflict resolved.

Asked to write a story based on her favourite reading, Esme in her first term at comprehensive school (Year 8, age 11–12) produced the following narrative about an elf called Bod (Figure 4.5). As in all children's work used as examples, I have corrected the original spelling and punctuation to allow the reader to concentrate on the structures of the story rather than other aspects of the writing.

My story: Bod

Bod was an elf, a lonely elf at that. His mother and father had given him away, sort of, like adopting.

His other mother, Jele, had told him that his parents had been very poor and they were starving and they did not want their baby to suffer. Eight megatrons (megatrons are like our six months) Bod had waited since that day until he was old enough to leave the underground world where they live and go out into the real world. He was 39 megatrons now, so he packed some things and left, leaving Jele and Mondrea, his other father, a note that read:

> Dear Jele and Mondrea,
> I am sorry, but I had to go. I have waited for four years to find my real mother and father and now I can. Don't worry I've packed a sensible bag and I'll be back as soon as possible.
> Lots of love,

'Oh, my little boy has gone,' Jele wept.
'Calm down, after all he is old enough. He wouldn't go if he wasn't, you know that,' Mondrea said, lying to calm her down.
'Yes, but it is a big world out there.'
'I know, Jele, I know.'
Jele started to cry again.

Meanwhile Bod was trying to convince the guard at the gate he was old enough to go. He had to show three forms of identification. He only had two, but just as he was about to be thrown out his best friend Quile came with four things in his hand. They were identification, one for Bod and three for him.
'Great, I would be glad of some company!'
Four weeks Bod and Quile had been travelling. Nothing, they found nothing.
'We'll never find them,' wept Bod.

'Hey Bod, it's all right. Hey, listen!'
'What!'
'Just listen.'
***
'The goblin's cave is where we live. We don't want elves around. We'll finish the elves' tunnel.'
'Oh no!'
'We'll have to save them.'
'Yes, but how?'
'We will have to tell the king.'
They caught a car (To catch a car you just jump on the bumper!) and went back to Elf land. Bod went into his house, Jele and Montrea were so glad to see him.
'Oh, my baby.'
'Listen, Jele.'
Bod told them about the goblins.
'Why didn't you carry on looking for your parents?'
'Because you and Mondrea raised me and as far as I am concerned, you're my parents.'
'What about the goblins?'
'Well I told the king and he said he'd handle it.'
'Oh, Bod.'
Bod went to fight the goblins when he was 47 megatrons and died fighting for his country.

The end

Esme's story begins effectively with an opening appropriate to younger children's stories. Esme seeks to orient her reader through establishing the main character, Bod's circumstances. The narrative stance she adopts in the first sentence is that of the omniscient narrator as guide; someone who knows all there is to know about the characters and whose comments will ensure that her reader can understand key points in the narrative, such as the meaning of 'megatrons'. This is a stance taken by many popular writers for the young. She skims over the need to establish the story's setting, allowing the names and the difference in the months to establish a different world for the reader. The names given the parents are generic ones, that is they establish a particular kind of context for the story without any descriptive detail or attention to character. They appear to be derived from science fiction stories whereas the main character's name has been taken from a television children's story. However the name also carries a generic meaning as 'a bod', a sort of everyman. Bod's quest to find his parents, accompanied by a faithful companion also has its origins in this genre, as does the episode where the goblins plan the elves' downfall in the tunnel. Esme's class has been reading the *The Hobbit* which has also influenced the association of tunnels and plotting goblins.

The first half of the narrative establishes the quest situation effectively but presents the reader with continuity problems in the second half where the sudden introduction of the goblin's conversation (marked in the text with

5·10·92

The story of how I learnt
to read

1 When I started to read, my mum and my Teacher
really helped alot so they in my life so I
could read books and signs on the street. If you
would like to read about school turn to 3, If you
would like to read about my favourite books turn
to 4.

2 All the books I've ever read have mainly come
from Librarys, friends, schools, shops, I mainly choose
them by looking at the cover or appearance. Mainly
my books all have a good cover or appearance, If
yoy would like to read about times and places
turn to 5

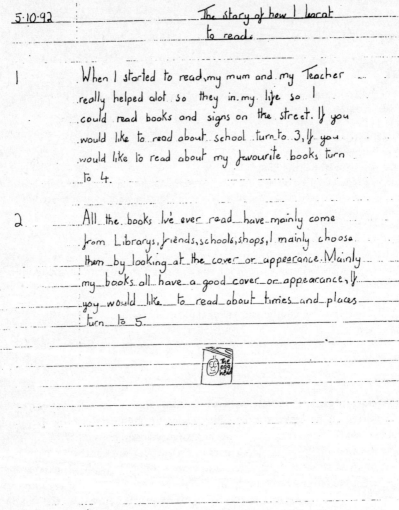

3 At my last school we had different kinds of reading
levels but I had past all the levels so I could
read anything in the class. The books I liked
in school were adventures the ones I didn't like
are sopy stories. Kinds of books The teachers read to
me are about children. If you havent already read
page 4 turn to that page. If you have turn to 5.

Figure 4.2 A fighting fantasy story format

4   When I was young my favourite book was
Thomas the Tank engine but now it is fighting
fantasy I like them because the book is different
every time you read the book. The people I read
my books with are my mum and friends
If you haven't already read about schools
to page 3, If you have turn to page 2

5

The times and places I read are usually
theres no one around and when its quite
I usually read in my bedroom. The pepple I
read to are my mum and mainly my teacher
If you haven't read page 2 turn to that
page if you have turn to page 6

6 My favourite comics and magazines are
Beano, Dandy, Lookin, Fast forwards My fave
characters are The Bash Street Kids
of the Beano and Roger the dodger
out of the Beano. Now turn to page 7

7 People (friends, Parents, Teachers,) have said to me
about my reading very good and the teacher
says my age group in reading is about 11-13.

Reading is brilliant when I find the right book.

Figure 4.2

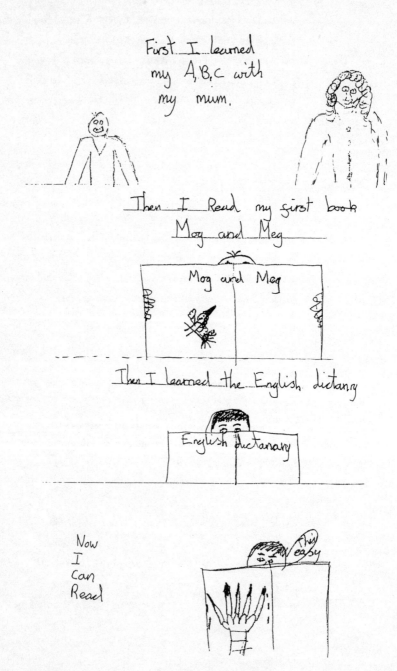

Story of Reading

First I learned
my A,B,C with
my mum.

Then I Read my first book
Mog and Meg

Mog and Meg

Then I learned the English dictany

English dictanary

Now
I
Can
Read

this
easy

Figures 4.3 and 4.4 The influence of comics

My favourite books are Sweet Valley Twins.
I like them because they are like
real life.
I share my books with my two
sisters and my friends.

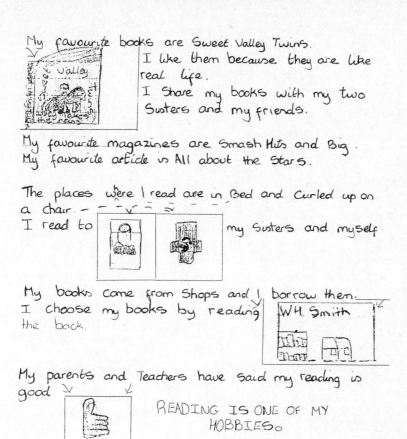

My favourite magazines are Smash Hits and Big.
My favourite article is All about the Stars.

The places were I read are in Bed and Curled up on
a chair.
I read to my sisters and myself.

My books come from Shops and I borrow them.
I choose my books by reading WH Smith
the back.

My parents and Teachers have said my reading is
good

READING IS ONE OF MY
HOBBIES.

Figure 4.4

MY STORY

Bod

Bod was an elf. Along elf at that. His mother and father had given him away sort of, like adopting. His other mother, Jele, had told him that his parents had been very poor and they were starving and they didn't want to [have baby to] [souver]. Eight megatons (megatons are like our sixmonths.) Bod had waited since that day until he was old enough to leave the underground world where they live and go out into the real world. He was 39 megatons now. So he packed some things and left leaving Jele and Mandrea his other father, a note that read:

Dear Jele and Mandrea,
I am sorry but i had to go I have waited for four years to pick my real mother and father and now I am. Be home soon love Jele. ... by now ill be as far as possible

which style?

"Oh my little boy has gone," Jele wept
"Calm down," after all he is old enough. He couldn't go if he wasn't, you know that" Mandrea said, trying to calm him down.
"yes, but it is a big cold out there."
"I know Jele, I know."
Jele started to cry again.
Meanwhile Bod was trying to courage he gard at the gate he was old enough to go. He had to show 3 forms of identification he only had 2. But just as he was about to be thrown out his best friend, Quile, came with 4 things in his hand. They were identification 1 for Bod and 3 for him.

Bod (continued)

"Great I could be glad of some company"
Four weeks Bod and Quile had been traveling, Nothing they found Nothing.
"We'll never find them,"wept Bod
"Hey Bod its alright. Hey listen"
"What?"
"Just listen"
"The Goblins cave is were we live we don't want elves around well finish the elves hund"
"Oh no"
"We'll have to save them"
"Yes but how"
"We call have to tell the king"
They caught a car (To catch a car you just jump on the bumper) and went 'back to Efe land Bod went into his house Jele and Mandrea were so glad to see him
"Oh, my baby"
"listen Jele"
Bod told them about the goblins
"Why didn't you carry on looking for your parents"
"Because you and mandrea raised me and as far as I'm concerned your my parents."
"What about the goblins"
"Well I told the king and he said hell handle it"
"Oh Bod"
(Bod went to fight the goblins when he was 47 megatons and Died fighting for his country

THE END

Figure 4.5 Esme's story of Bod

asterisks) is introduced without any exposition to guide the reader as to who is speaking and whom they are addressing. It is typical of a large number of children's writing in that it uses dialogue to comment on the action while speeding it up. Such dialogue is frequently substituted for a detailed account of key events and again reflects the influence of television cartoons and comic strips. It is as if the writer is visualizing a set of picture images, as one might on a story board, to create a commentary about something that has not been fully realized in words.

Moreover, although the events described in *Bod* have their starting point in the quest story, with characters out adventuring on their own, searching for a lost parent and saving a nation from goblin attack, these themes are not very well developed. Instead, it is the cosy world of a girls' magazine story with its concentration on the necessity of looking after others and a coda about the nature of a true parent, which structures the story's main closure. Opportunities for developing the description of a heroic struggle with the goblins, which forms the story's main complication, are side-stepped although the opening context set up expectations of such a struggle.

As Janet White who has studied the differences found in girls' and boys' narratives has shown in her analysis of the stories adolescents adapt for younger children (Carter, 1990: 181–97):

> Girls don't like to write about mindless fighting and killing . . . and consequently seek to minimise such episodes in their stories.

The result of this side-stepping in Esme's story is a certain flatness of tone and an impression of premature closure. Esme has not fully understood the episodic nature of the quest genre but has settled for a conventional reconciliation between parent and child as her main narrative focus.

A more confusing story, resulting from a mixture of styles, which also appear to combine the strategies of written and visual narratives, is found in David's piece, which he also wrote as an illustration of the kind of story he most enjoys (Figure 4.6).

The Alien that came to Earth

Once an alien called Miss Bash was screwing around in outer space. She lived on the planet Garcon, when suddenly her ship went out of control.

As she went down, down, and down she passed the heat barrier and came into Earth and landed in a bunch of English grown cactus. She shot out of the window and into a holly bush and she ran into a playground full of children, rummaging around in the playground, boys kicking a football, girls skipping.

The alien said to a boy where am I? and the young boy said well, just about to say it and a young yob said glasses had gone away. The alien said funny.

David opens his story clearly enough, orienting his reader by introducing a character and creating a setting, even if the details are a little perfunctory. For

The Alien that came to erth

Once an Alien callde Miss Bash was
screwing around in outer space. She lived in
the planet garcon when Sundenley her ship
whent out of control.
As She whet dom dome dom She past the
heat barega e cam into erth. And landed in a
bonch of English grown cattus. She shout
out of the windom and into hollybush.
And She ran into a play grounde full of
chilldren romeging around in the play graunde
bouyo kicing a ball girlls skiping
The alien sed to a boy when am I
and the youg the youn sed well, gust about
to say it.
And a younge yobe sed glassos head
goome away the alien sed juny.

Figure 4.6 David's story, *The alien*

example the name Miss Bash coupled to a planet 'Garcon', may be drawing on a school context which David expects his readers to share, a French teacher, perhaps, so that the character is left as a 'generic' without further description to help the reader.

The complication in this story is the crash landing of the spaceship. As in Esme's story, the use of dialogue creates most confusion for the reader. The conversation is very difficult to follow because as well as lack of appropriate punctuation and setting out, David does not establish the relationship between the people speaking or their response to each other's utterances. This results in a very unsatisfactory resolution of the conflict with no clear indication whether the problem has been solved.

The model for the writing again seems to be a comic strip or television cartoon. This view is supported by the writer's choice of language such as 'screwing', the use of slap-stick humour, 'landed in a bunch of English grown cactus' and the clever-comment ending, 'funny'. The situation has been visualized rather than fully explicated so that a reader would require more commentary to be able to judge the characters' responses to each other and ultimately to understand what has happened.

Both these stories raise the question of what teachers expect from children when they ask them to write a story. The question becomes an even more important issue when we consider that story writing is the most frequent genre of composition asked from children by schools.

When Peter Medway analysed the writing tasks set for 12-year olds by their secondary English teachers in a northern city he found that 46 per cent of the written outcomes could be described as fiction and a further 15 per cent as personal writing and concluded that they were experiencing a version of English dominated by stories which 'demanded an aesthetic reading' (Sheeran and Barnes, 1991: 84).

Genre studies of early children's writing particularly studies conducted in Australia (Martin, 1985) have argued that all writing begins in the form of personal recount, that is an account or comment on things that have been experienced and that these accounts gradually differentiate into narrative and report modes. The ability of children to adapt their first compositions to more recognizable written forms depends on their familiarity with written rather than spoken narratives.

Stories are culturally determined and follow particular rules and conventions. Children learn these rules through exposure to, and familiarity with, the different genres. Written stories need a written model rather than the visual and auditory models presented by the film, television and computer game narratives with which many of them are now more familiar. In the following examples pupils have been given more particular frameworks. Mark wrote the following story at the same stage of development as David and at the same time in the school term, September, just after he had moved to the secondary school. The narrative is preceded by his first attempt at writing in his new school (Figure 4.7).

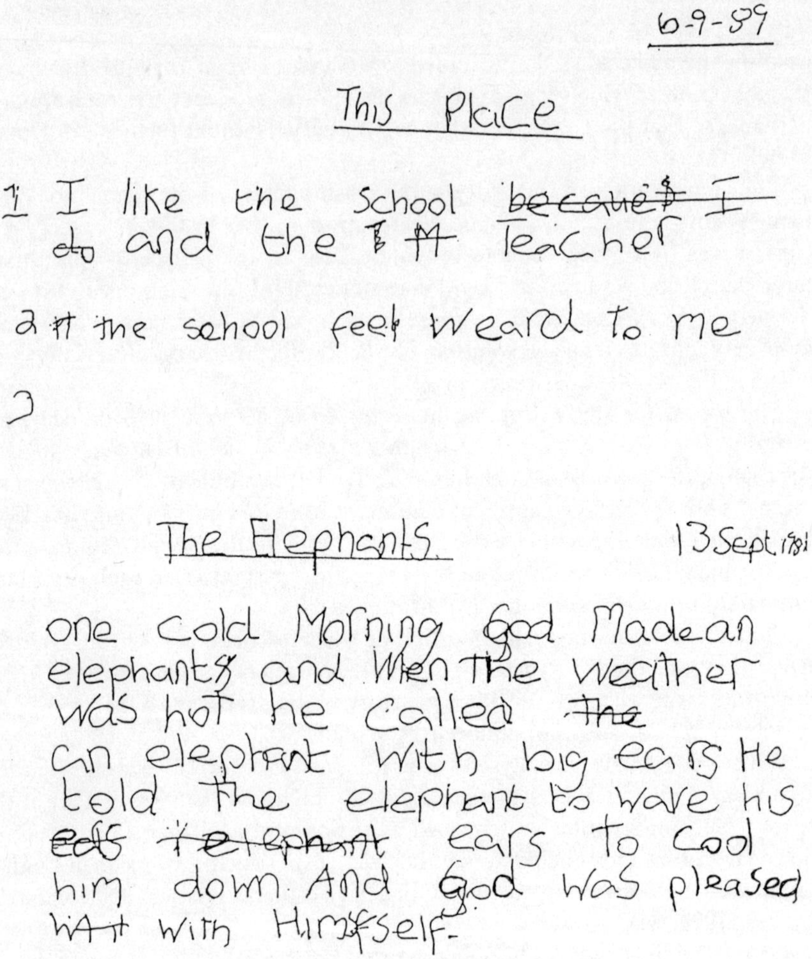

6-9-89

<u>This Place</u>

1 I like the school ~~because I~~
~~do~~ and the ~~t~~ ~~ft~~ Teacher

a ~~ft~~ the school feel weard to me

)

<u>The Elephants.</u>   13 Sept 1981

one cold Morning God Made an
elephants and When the weather
Was hot he called ~~the~~
an elephant With big ears He
told the elephant to wave his
~~ears~~ ~~t elephant~~ ears to cool
him down. And God was pleased
~~wit~~ with Himself.

Figure 4.7 *The elephants.* Note how hesitantly Mark approaches his first writing task, *This place*

This Place

1. I like the school ~~because I do~~ and the teacher.
2. the school feel weird to me.
3.

The Elephants

One cold morning God made an elephant and when the weather was hot he called an elephant with big ears. He told the elephants to wave his ears to cool him down. And God was pleased with Himself.

Mark's elephant story may at a glance seem less well developed than David's story about the alien. The piece is much shorter, Mark's sentences are simpler in construction and he has not completed an earlier attempt to write about his new school. In fact the latter piece, written on the second day of the term, shows very clearly that Mark does not find writing easy. He has tried to complete the set task in a conventional way by expressing approval of his new school, particularly of the teachers but the attempt has collapsed and we sense his total bewilderment. Yet when his Elephant story is read aloud, the reader is immediately struck by its completeness. The writing has a gnomic quality appropriate to a creation myth and the language of fable. Mark's new-found fluency can be directly attributed to his teacher having read some of Ted Hughes' creation stories from *How the Whale Became* and *Tales of the Early World* and the discussion which preceded the writing. Perhaps one sentence in particular from the Ted Hughes story, *How the Elephant Became*, has influenced his writing. Hughes describes the elephant as 'having great ears that flapped and hung' and this is the central feature of Mark's version. Knowledge of the Bible creation story and its phraseology also add to the effect.

> And God made the beast of the earth after his kind, and cattle after their kind, and everything that creepeth upon the earth after his kind, and God saw that it was good.
>
> *Genesis*, 1 v. 22

The shape of the Bible story also acts to support Mark's writing, allowing him to complete this piece of work successfully. In the next example, by a very competent Y7 writer, Richard, the influence of the Hughes model is even more evident (Figure 4.8).

Why the Polar Bear is Pure White

When God created the animals he created the polar bear first.
   'My first animal shall be the greatest of them all, therefore he shall have the brightest colours,' God said. He placed him carefully on the earth and set him off on his way. Five days later (when all the animals had been made) the polar bear saw how brightly coloured he was, compared to all the others. He stuck his

Why the polar bear is pure white   11 September 1989

When God created the animals, he created the polar bear first. "My first animal shall be the greatest of them all; thereifor he shall have the brightest coulours" God said. He placed him carefully on the earths and set him off on his way. Five days later (when all the animals were made) the polar bear saw how brightly coulourod he was compared to all the others. He stuck his nose up in the air, and turned around as he said "I'm not staying around with all of you lot. You're all too common and short of coulours. Where as i'm bright and brilliant!" and ×Whx with that he walked away. All of the other animals were shocked and annoyed at this, so the lion, (the leader of them all), decided to have a meeting. "We are gathered here, to descuss what to do about the polar bear," The lion said "He's so stuck up!" Squarked the parrot. And all of the other animals agreed. "I surgest," continued the lion. "That we play some sort of trick on him for his selfishness, But what can we do?"

There was a short pause and then the monkey ×Shox said "I've got it! we will hide behind a ×rotten rock, with a white sheet over us, and then jump out at him, Making horrible noises! That shold scare him silly!!" and the animals agreed ×Thenx that that was what they'd do. So in the morning, as the polar bear was taking his morning walk, admiring himself by the river they all jumped out at him. The polar bear was so frightened, that he froze in shock and went totally white. God had seen all of this, so he called out with a boom –

"Polar bear, you have been so snobby, selfish, immature, and such a show off. for that reson, your punishment will be, to be totally white forever!" And that is why the polar bear is pure white to this day.

Figure 4.8 *Why the polar bear is pure white*

nose up in the air and turned around as he said, 'I am not staying around with all of you lot. You're all too common and short of colours, whereas I'm bright and brilliant!' and with that he walked away. All of the other animals were shocked and annoyed at this, so the lion (the leader of them all) decided to have a meeting.

'We are gathered here to discuss what to do about the polar bear,' the lion said.

'He's *so* stuck-up!' squawked the parrot, and all the other animals agreed.

'I suggest,' continued the lion, 'that we play some kind of trick on him for his selfishness, but what shall we do?'

There was a short pause and then the monkey said, 'I've got it, we'll hide behind a rock with a white sheet over us and then jump out at him, making horrible noises! That should scare him silly!!!', and the animals agreed that was what they'd do. So in the morning, as the polar bear was taking his morning walk admiring himself by the river, they all jumped out at him. The polar bear was so frightened, that he froze in shock and went totally white. God had seen all of this and called out with a boom,

'Polar bear you have been so snobby, selfish, immature and such a show-off, for that reason your punishment will be to be totally white for ever.'

And that is why the polar bear is pure white to this day.

This second example shows clearly how the writer's knowledge of the Hughes' story acts as a sustaining form behind the creation of a new story. The writing achieves its effects so cleverly that some teachers on first seeing it suggest that the work has been copied. In fact, it is the style rather than the content that has been imitated and made the writer's own. Hughes' version of the Polar Bear story has the bear proud of her white coat, voluntarily banishing herself to the northern snow to avoid the dirt. Richard's story reverses the process using 'whiteness' as the animal's punishment for pride, with associations of deprivation and lack of colour rather than the conventional ones of purity or supremacy. Richard has grasped the role of rhetoric in establishing leadership and managing the masses. The story has the simple moralizing conclusion appropriate to an animal fable and the story is altogether perfectly realized.

Other ways in which writers can be helped to use their knowledge of storybook language to increase their understanding of story structure is by letting them analyse the recurrent aspects of a particular genre and incorporate some of these aspects into the stories they produce. Traditional stories make a good starting point for this work as many of their characteristics form the stuff of fictions in other media so that children can begin to explore their contents with confidence. For example, the *Cinderella* and *Puss in Boots* theme of rags to riches, although offering differing routes for boys and girls, is the central motif of much nineteenth century literature. Equally the quest for something missing or stolen, sustains much fantasy writing, including the Games Workshop adventure books and the interactive video games that are very popular at this age. One Year 6 class began a story writing project by reading widely from a collection of traditional and folk tales, including some modern story versions such as *The Practical Princess* and *There's a Wolf in My Pudding*. They then worked in groups to categorize the most common features of these stories.

Group one: They listed the main characters in such stories such as woodcutter's families, youngest sons, poor boys, servant girls, princesses, soldiers, three brothers or sisters, knights, a frog.

Group two: They looked for the people who opposed the central character, such as wicked uncles, stepmothers, witches, cruel rulers, wizards, a dragon.

Group three: They looked for magic objects that helped on the quest, seven-league boots, talking animals, magic pots, tinder boxes, swords, golden apples, magic wands, cloaks to make you invisible.

Group four: They looked for the reward at the end of the story, a princesses' hand in marriage, treasure, rule of the kingdom, banishment for the evil character.

Group five: They looked for settings and their descriptions suggesting forests, castles, dungeons, cottages, ice kingdoms, under the sea, enchanted gardens.

The groups then pooled their ideas and created a databank of story constituents and by making choices from this bank of story possibilities they were able to work in small groups of three or four to create stories which followed a traditional pattern with some new elements added. The following is part of one of the completed tales which was composed, word processed, illustrated and finally included in a class collection of short stories, called *Seven from Class Seven* (Figure 4.9).

Jack Strikes It Lucky

Jack was an orphan. He had never known his parents. He had been abandoned in the woods and found in a cardboard box. His only possessions were a dummy and a small dagger. He was looked after by a kind woodcutter but when Jack was only six years old, the woodcutter died after a nasty accident with an axe, and Jack had to go back to living in a cardboard box. *As Jack grew older he became more sensitive about his situation.* He did not like being a young tramp, but he had no choice. He befriended a stray dog that wandered about looking for scraps of food. Jack had no idea what an ordinary life was like. When Jack was a little boy the woodcutter had told Jack that his dagger looked very expensive, but it had a diamond missing. The woodcutter thought that if he could get a diamond to fit in the dagger it might be magic.

'How could I possibly get a diamond,' thought Jack to himself as he huddled up in his cardboard box.

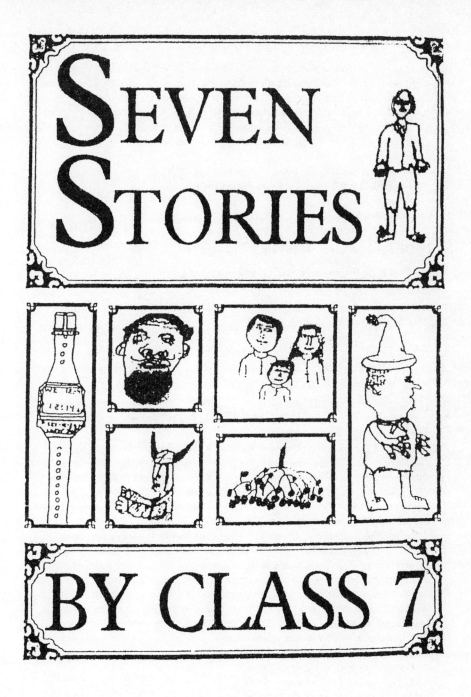

Figure 4.9 Cover from *Seven from Class Seven*

Suddenly there was a large bang on the side of the box. Jack was scared, so he drew his dagger from his dagger holder. He burst open the box but to his amazement, towering above him were three Royal Guards.

The commander said, 'What's your name then?' There was no answer. Jack was speechless. He did not know what to say to the guards.

'We are the king's Royal Guards. Are you a tramp?'

'What if I am?'

'There is a message for you.'

Jack said, 'I can't read. Can you read it for me?'

'All right then.'

Dear Homeless and Penniless,

This is an Invitation to the Tramps' Banquet being held at the King's palace tomorrow at 12 noon.

signed,

King Richard of Hernia.

'Do you know any more tramps round here?'

'No' said Jack, and the guards marched off. So the next morning Jack set off past the misty swamps and old gold mines. He finally reached the palace where all the other tramps were waiting.

When all the tramps had arrived the king's guard opened the big black doors and there stood the king, dressed in his golden cloak that shone like the sun. All the tramps bowed down to their great and powerful monarch. In his powerful voice the king made an announcement: 'Eat all the food you want.' All the tramps rushed into the dining hall. *They were speechless when they saw turkeys on the table and they were flabbergasted when champagne was poured into their glasses.* Although the king seemed friendly, he had been known to chop a few heads off in his time. Then in a flash of light one of the tramps dived on to the table and ripped off his disguise. It was a demon! He was covered in red scales and had horrible teeth. *All the tramps were so scared they dived under the tables. The* demon leapt on the king and forced his crown off his head. The king shouted, 'Guard the doors!' The guards held their axes up high to try to trap the demon, but the king forgot about the bedroom. So the demon dashed into the king's bedroom. The queen screamed and said: 'How dare you come into my bedroom without knocking. I will have your head off for this!'

The demon said, 'Shut up, Queen.'

The king shed a few tears, then sighed and said, 'Is there anyone brave enough to regain my crown? If anyone can complete this quest, I solemnly swear they can marry my youngest and most beautiful daughter, plus half of my kingdom, but if they fail they will be fed to the crocodiles.' There was a long silence in the crowded dining hall. None of the other tramps wanted to do it. So Jack decided to have a go himself. It was his chance to be rich and to stop living in a cardboard box. *He knew he could conquer the demon with his dagger, which was supposed to be magic, but he needed to find that one missing diamond to fit in the hole.* Surely the king would lend him a diamond? It was worth a try for half of the kingdom and the hand of a princess.

Jack stood up, his knees knocking.

'I'll do it your majesty.' All the tramps gasped, then laughed. One shouted out, 'A little boy like that! He couldn't kill a fly, even if he tried.' But Jack slowly walked forward with all the tramps laughing at him. The king shouted, 'Silence or I will have your heads off.' Jack carried on walking and trembling. When he got to the solid gold chair where the king was sitting he whispered in his ear, 'May I have one wish and a word in private?'

The king said, 'Yes my boy, anything you need for this dangerous mission, as long as you get my crown back.'

Jack said to the king, 'Could I possibly borrow a small diamond to fit in my dagger?'

The king sent for a guard and ordered, 'Fetch some pliers and that old crown from the cellar.' The king asked for Jack's dagger. It was stuffed down his sock, so he pulled it out of his sock full of holes and passed it to the king. The guard returned with an old crown, and the king pulled out a diamond and managed to fit it in the handle of the dagger. Jack took the dagger off the king. The beautiful diamond glinted in the light. He knew it was magic. *All of a sudden, a flash of lightning struck outside the palace, and then, out of the dagger sprung two handles and the blade grew bigger and bigger to form itself into a sword.* Jack's dream had come true. The dagger was magic after all.

The story continues for several more pages, but it easy to see how the plot will develop. It is a lengthy piece that clearly shows how a modelling of what a reader might expect from a particular piece of writing, coupled to a drafting process in which readers' views are consulted, has allowed these pupils to extend their narrative competencies. The story is much more developed than the narratives produced by Esme and David who chose their own story models and wrote without conferencing or drafting, except to proofread for spelling and punctuation. The writing also shows fairly sophisticated linguistic competence which has been stressed in the rewrite of the National Curriculum. The writers have used a range of connectives in complex sentences with subordinate clauses (see the sentences in italics in the story printed above). There is a preponderance of simple sentences but there are also sentences that effectively use antithesis, inversion and a range of subordinate structures. The elements from traditional stories that the group has chosen for their story are obvious. They include the transformation of the fortunes of a boy of humble origin, the use of a magic object to defeat a supernatural enemy, the completion of a difficult task by the least likely contestant, and the gaining of reward that includes both a share in the kingdom and the princess's hand in marriage.

There are elements that are typical of this age group's unguided narratives too; such as the rapid, rather knock-about actions following the demon's appearance and the use of contemporary tramps. That these are subordinated to elements that suggest familiarity with the written conventions of narrative form is shown firstly in the conciseness of exposition, in sentences such as: 'but when Jack was only six years old, the woodcutter died after a nasty accident with an axe, and Jack had to go back to living in a cardboard box.' and also in the ability to account for Jack's thoughts and feelings in an indirect manner: 'So Jack decided to have a go himself.'

This was his chance to be rich and to stop living in a cardboard box. He knew he could conquer the demon with his dagger which was supposed to be magic, but he needed to find that one missing diamond to fit in the hole. Surely the king would lend him a diamond? It was worth a try for half of the kingdom and the hand of a princess. Because the story is based on a study of a genre, rather than an individual tale, it is more difficult to pin-point direct evidence of responses to particular texts as a reader can in Hugh's story, quoted at the beginning of the chapter. However there is a particular texture of writing and a familiarity with narrative technique that suggests informed understanding of the form. This understanding can be further developed at a latter stage when the class have become so familiar with a particular narrative that they are able to parody it.

One example of this is provided by a Y7 group's work that developed after reading *The Wolf Has His Say*, a parody of the Little Red Riding Hood story included in the collection and *There's a Wolf in My Pudding*, by David Henry Wilson, in which the wolf posthumously offers a defence of his actions, accusing both little Red Riding Hood and her grandmother of deception.

After a lesson spent reading the text closely for supporting evidence, the class organized a trial of the wolf to put the case for both the prosecution and defence, allowing 12 jurors to make a final judgement on the defendant's guilt. They then looked at other stories where a particular character was cast in the role of the villain which they might retell from an alternative point of view. One of these was at the story of Circe and Odysseus which they retold from the point of view of the sorceress, with results that showed their understanding not only of the story's content, but also their grasp of the idea of an alibi that might not stand up to very close scrutiny. Emma's version begins:

> My name is Circe. History has painted a false picture of me, but if you will allow I would like to tell the true story. The day had been stormy but now it was warm and sunny and I was sitting in my conservatory when a troop of men rampaged through my back garden. They looked tired and hungry so naturally I offered them lunch. I didn't drug anything. It was all the fault of the cook. She had drugged the men's soup as her husband, the gardener, intended to rob them. After lunch they were staggering about so just for a laugh I turned them into pigs, as all men are anyway!
>
> How was I to know there was someone else hiding in the room, who thought I was a big bad witch who turned men to pigs for fun?

The story has an assured narrative tone. Emma quickly sets the scene with a few brief descriptive details and begins her account with a coda that shows her purpose is to convince her reader of her version of events. She ends her story of the Odysseus's sojourn in this way:

> I then asked Odysseus if he would be my boy-friend. He agreed but only because my father owned the only hotel on the island. Anyway, how do you think I felt when he ran off like that, after only one year? Sad? Not likely, I was glad to see him go. I gave him the directions. I thought of giving him the wrong ones, but I didn't though, in case he ended up back here. Now, that's the true story and do not believe anything else you hear, because it is false.

Emma has taken her narrative frame from the David Henry Wilson story and used it to rework the myth she has heard in class. Knowledge of both stories allows her to make a personal statement about the duplicity involved in the Circe and Odysseus relationship in an amusing way. Her story engages the reader's interest because of the skill in retelling rather than an originality of events or fertility of imagination.

In a recent study of writing across the secondary curriculum, Douglas Barnes and Yanina Sheeran have drawn teachers' attention to what they have identified as the 'ground rules of writing' which operate in different curriculum areas. They attempt to make explicit the often implicit criteria on which teachers judge the performance of their pupils in specific curriculum contexts (Sheeran and Barnes, 1991). In the discussion of writing in secondary English lessons they point out that teachers frequently rely on a literary stimulus as a model for the starting point of writing, further suggesting that even the themes that are presented as personal writing depend largely on literary representations of appropriate ideas and feelings in particular contexts. In judging writing, it is the shaping of the experience that is more important than the raw experience itself. How can it be otherwise, for to judge the work on the quality of the experience would imply that those pupils with the most interesting lives would be the most successful writers. Implicit in the work set for English lessons is the teacher's expectation that the writer will use appropriate forms. On one level, Barnes and Sheeran suggests writing in English may ignore the conscious teaching of methods of structuring ideas, instead relying on the emerging purposes of the individual writer to find an appropriate form. They suggest that (ibid., 1991: 98):

> the skill and deliberate planning required by many kinds of writing have been undervalued in the interests of direct outpourings in which the writer is writing primarily for him or herself. This kind of writing – intended for no one else but the sympathetic eye of the English teacher.

Their case is a little overstated. Writing in less personal formats is the accepted mode of most other subject areas and the attempt to shape personal experience to share with others, even if it is your English teacher, allows for the development of new forms of expression. Work in English has also stressed the importance of audience for writing in a consistent way not fully acknowledged by this analysis. Not only have coursework criteria for public examinations at 16 years stressed from the outset the importance of writing in a variety of forms, but also the National Curriculum Attainment Targets for Writing (DES, 1989) include a requirement both to draft work and to write for specific audiences from an early starting point.

Sheeran and Barnes however also suggest that such implicit ground rules of writing are so familiar to the teachers that they may adopt an

'intuitive' model of language teaching across the curriculum.

Further (ibid., 1991: 114):

By this we mean that the rules of the writing game are largely left unspoken and it is assumed that the learners will absorb what they need to know.

I have found in listening to, and reading a good many stories, told and written by children at both sides of the transition from primary to secondary school, that unless the teacher draws their attention to story form as an integral and explicit part of the learning process, many children with limited personal experience of reading fall back on other genre forms to organize their narratives. These are mainly the visual genres most familiar to them from popular culture. This results in a lack of focus and textual organization as demonstrated in Esme's and David's stories. It also reinforces the gender differences as I intend to illustrate in the following chapter. When children are expected to explore different kinds of story together as part of their reading and then encouraged to discuss their responses in conference sessions, there is a corresponding development in their own writing. The essential focus for structuring writing through the introduction of a wide range of story genre is that the teacher emphasizes the importance of the effect on a reader's understanding rather than analysing structural elements for their own sake.

There is a new emphasis in the re-write of the English National Curriculum (DES, 1993) on recommended reading for each stage of development and on the syntactical elements of correct composition. Both these changes may result in a more formal approach to presenting fiction in school. There are several problems arising from this as, although the majority of the books recommended are ones that teachers would happily include in their class libraries, they may now be treated as objects for analysis rather than integrated into a whole-language approach to reading and writing. Moreover, teachers anxious to teach 'about' language (for example, it is suggested children should be taught the difference between a noun and a clause) may return to the mechanistic exercises provided by published, structured language schemes that are already widely available. The ability to 'recognize' and label language structures is far less important than using them successfully in writing and understanding their role in constructing meaning.

Implications for the reading curriculum

1 Children's implicit understanding of plot and character may not have been derived from print narratives. They need to encounter a wide variety of written genre to understand how to shape their own writing.

2 Teachers can create a learning context in which reading and writing of narrative promotes children's understanding of language in the following ways:

   (i) Choose stories to share in class which introduce particular narrative structures and through close reading help pupils to understand their effects on the person reading. These should include some picture stories where narrative devices are often more obvious as well as texts which parody or give alternative versions of well-known genres.

  (ii) When setting written assignments, be explicit about the kind of narrative writing required rather than relying on children's implicit understanding of the story genre.

 (iii) Allow time for conferencing where children can discuss each other's writing and help each other with the cohesion of narratives by locating places where a reader needs more information to follow the story or understand a character's motivation.

 (iv) Draw the class's attention to particular stories and other pupils' work in which particular narrative devices have been used effectively.

  (v) Use pupils' written narrative work as a diagnostic tool for assessing their level of understanding of story and to help them to identify ways to improve their own composition.

5 Reading choice: a question of gender?

Boys exult in superhuman strength, girls seek gentle relationships. Boys talk of blood and mayhem, girls avoid the subject. A character in a girl's story simply dies, no details given. Boys fly, leap, crash and dive. Girls have picnics and brush their teeth; the meanest ugliest character in a girl's story goes on picnics and keeps his teeth clean.

Vivian Gussi Paley

Boys are more likely than girls to be the centre of attention in a class. Through blood and guts narration they are singled out and reprimanded by their teacher. Similarly their serialised narratives may be banned. On the positive side, their cartoons and spoofs may bring them the admiration of all concerned. Successful girls' narrative, reflective and caring as it often is, tends to draw a less public response from the teacher – an encouraging written comment or a word of quiet praise.

J.R. Martin

Boys and girls continue to grow up with very different models of the kinds of behaviour that is appropriate to their gender role. Schools reflect society's expectation that they should have different educational aspirations, even reinforcing these differences by the choices they offer and the options they suggest each follow. These school influences are now well documented as evidenced in recent collections of research data from primary and secondary schools (Delamont, 1990; Minns, 1991). In Western societies, reading is presented largely as a girl-preferred activity. Girls are more likely to be shown as readers in the illustrations in children's books, given books as presents for birthdays and Christmas and describe themselves as devoted to their books (Willinsky and Hunniford, 1993: 92).

As children mature, gender differences become more marked and habits more firmly established, so that some behaviours associated with one sex become taboo for the other. Studies have shown that, in their early years at home or at playschool, girls are more likely to be encouraged to participate in quieter, more passive activities in private spaces such as colouring, cutting out and reading by themselves; whilst boys have more interactive toys such as Lego and Stickle Bricks and are encouraged in boisterous games. Analysis of the kinds of play encouraged by toys such as Action Man, My Little Pony, war toys, replicas of home appliances and many others suggest playthings marketed for boys encourage louder, more aggressive and confrontational play, where-as girls' toys encourage co-operation and quiet simulations. The processes of aculturation are largely hidden, supported by patterns of gift buying and friendship grouping that reinforce expectations of certain preferences or be-haviours. For example, some of the play activities designed by Lego have focused on domestic interiors, and these sets are more often bought for nieces and granddaughters than the machines, space stations, vehicles and larger scale buildings, favoured by boys.

Moreover, activities that are seen as girl-preferred are surrounded with far more taboos for boys than boy-preferred activities are for the girls. Dressing in 'male attire', acquiring boys' toys, and 'trying on' a male role is part of most girl's early experience. The role models they encounter reinforce the positive aspects of masculinity, whether these are represented by dramatic roles, such as in Shakespeare's Rosalind or Shaw's *St Joan* or those suggested by the casual adoption of jeans, tee shirts and boots. The female role, on the other hand, is always an area that acts as transgressive for boys, an area for disquiet or ridicule as represented in the roles of Dame Edna Everidge or the pantomime dame. Boys call each other 'girl' or 'girlie', or, even 'big soft lass', if they wish to demean each other, whereas tomboys are an accepted part of female culture and presented positively in young women's literature. Louisa Alcott's Jo, cited by many successful women as their favourite character, is a prime example of this particular role model.

In a recent role-play activity devised for English teachers in training, a group was asked to work on Shakespearean insults from the perspective of the other gender. The women students fell readily into representations of male language (in this case Capulets and Montagues abusing each other as if they were rival fans in a football crowd) whereas the men were unable to sustain their female roles (Hermione insulting Hermia) without the use of false voices and dressing-up clothes. The men took longer to devise their short scene and obviously felt ill at ease in adopting the female roles without the mask provided by a change in voice and appearance.

I use the example of cross-dressing with purpose, because the act of reading in the middle years can be characterized as a trying on of role through identi-fication with the actions of a particular character in a story. J.A. Appleyard in his developmental study of the growth of the reader (1990: 57–93), labels this stage of later childhood or pre-teens, 'Reader as Hero and Heroine', suggesting that 'the distinctive role readers take at this stage is to imagine themselves as heroes and heroines of romances that are unconscious analogues of their own lives'. In fact, what young readers look for in the texts they explore are models of the kinds of adults or adult behaviour they aspire to become. Many girls choose to read books with male heroes because the qualities of bravery and resistance are important to their view of themselves; few boys choose to read books with women at the centre. Appleyard further suggests (ibid.: 92–3) that at this stage their interests meet in the Romance genre or quest story where both the need for adventure and the working out of relationships is possible.

At the transition stage of schooling, adolescents have a growing divergence of interests and boys become anxious to dissociate themselves from any of the activities they believe to be favoured by girls, even when they had previously joined in with mixed groups without hesitation. Because boys have an over-whelming need not to be seen as 'girlish', it is important that books in school should be presented in ways which make them equally attractive to both sexes if both are to be given equal access to the power that comes from being a flexible reader. This poses a difficulty for teachers wishing to share books with whole classes because a pattern of gender differentiation is clearly discernible in their pupils' attitudes to, and choice of, popular reading at all stages. When a boy calls a girl's book 'soppy' he is declaring that its subject matter, often about relationships and romance, hold no interest or relevance for him whereas girls will read books with boys as the main character time and again in school with little sense of injustice.

The reaction I recorded as a classroom teacher of a bright boy in a first-year class to my introduction *Private Keep Out*, by Gwen Grant, a book with a female central character, is fairly typical of this feeling. The story has a boisterous working-class girl at its centre recounting stories of her large family through the medium of a diary. After hearing one chapter, Alan wrote this in the reading journal we used to record and share response (Millard, 1985: 60):

> Dear Mrs Millard,
> About the book PKO. I think it is very boring. If you must read something, read something more interesting. Why can't Mrs Loughran read the boys a story and you read the girls PKO?

Appleyard's categorization of the stages of response to story have helped me to understand that the realistic genre of this particular story, with its emphasis on believable characters and everyday situations did not allow the whole class to identify with the action of the characters when the central character was a girl.

Popular authors understand the importance of psychological identification perfectly and where they direct their stories at both sexes the characters usually provide the readers with very carefully differentiated sex roles. For example, in Enid Blyton's *Famous Five* series, it is Dick who takes the lead, supported by Julian, while Anne sounds the notes of caution like a little mother and George, as tomboy, allows some girls an appropriately adventurous role model. Wendy mothers Peter Pan and the lost boys while also serving as the damsel in distress for them to rescue, Peter Rabbit defies Mr Macgregor whilst his little sisters are good and stay home. Although Flopsy, Mopsy and Cotton Tail are not ascribed a gender by the text the illustrations in the original editions show them clothed in pink cloaks, always a female signifier, whilst Peter has a blue coat and shoes. Roald Dahl's characters are obnoxious in a sex-differentiated ways with the most unpleasant roles in all the stories reserved for older females.

In the past, reading schemes, attempting to cater for both sexes, have emphasized the differences, rather than the similarities, in boys' and girls' interests, a characteristic beautifully parodied in this 12-year-old's version of Ladybird's Peter and Jane (Nicholas and Collette) which shows clearly how children fully understand the limitations of the worlds that such reading schemes create for them.

Collette and Nicholas go to the park

N: Today we shall go to the park, Collette, today we shall go to the park.
C: Oh yes, Nicholas, oh yes!
N: What shall we take with us, Collette, what shall we take with us?
C: Shall we take some *egg* sandwiches, Nicholas, shall we take some *egg* sandwiches?

N: No, you know what they do to me, Collette, you know what they do to me.
C: Oh I forgot, Nicholas, I forgot.
N: We shall take some *ham* sandwiches, Collette, we shall take *ham* sandwiches.
C: All right, Nicholas, all right.

At the park

N: Look at the swings, Collette, look at the swings.
C: Can I play on the swings, Nicholas, can I play on the swings?
N: No, set out the sandwiches, Collette, set out the sandwiches!
C: All right, Nicholas, all right.

N: I'm going to play on the rocks, Collette, I'm going to play on the rocks.
C: All right, Nicholas, all right.
N: Watch me play on the rocks, Collette, watch me play on the rocks!
C: Wonderful, Nicholas, Wonderful!

N: I've fallen off the rocks, Collette, I've fallen off the rocks.
C: You poor boy, Nicholas, you poor boy.
N: I've fallen in the river, Collette, I've fallen in the river.
C: But Daddy only taught you to swim, Nicholas, Daddy only taught you to swim.

N: I think I'm going to drown, Collette, I think I'm going to drown.
C: Are you really, Nicholas, are you really?
N: Blub! Blub! Blub! Collette, Blub! Blub! Blub!
C: Oh dear, what shall I tell Mummy, Nicholas, what shall I tell Mummy?

The end

Modern reading schemes, such as *The Oxford Reading Tree* have tried to take account of such sex-differentiated interest, but they have probably moved in the wrong direction. Main characters, like Bif and Kipper, have names and styles of clothing are so unisex that they confuse the reader about their actual gender and therefore weaken the sense of up-to-the-minute realism which the scheme hopes to create.

In the first year of secondary school, mixed classrooms are found to offer books that are mainly about boys, or girls masquerading as boys until the final pages, as for example in the case of the eponymous heroine of Gene Kemp's *The Turbulent Term of Tyke Tyler*, whose tomboy habits and ambiguous name coupled with Kemp's avoidance of third person pronouns in the text, hide her femaleness until the last chapter. One teacher analysing the role of 'positive female characters' in literature recommended as being non-sexist concluded that these books appeared to be those in which:

• Girls were given aggressive or boyish characters.
• Girls were shown having a really bad time because they were girls.
• Girls were just as powerful as boys and had the same interests, particularly football.
• Girls liked wearing scruffy clothes and building go-karts.
• Girls picked on wimpish boys and stupid princes.
• Girls had butch nicknames that could just as easily belong to a boy, e.g. Biff, Tyke.

She also concluded that these were messages hardly likely to win over the girls or make them more confident in their femininity. However, because these non-sexist books are not widely used in schools, they probably create an interesting point of contrast when encountered rather than acting as wish fulfilment. More typical is the Edinburgh study of classroom work with fiction which reported that (Riddell, 1989: 183–97):

> In English lessons, almost all the books which were used featured boys as the main characters, often dealing with the problems of the male adolescent. When I discussed this with one particular English teacher she said this had never occurred to her before, but it was clearly not fair: 'We certainly wouldn't expect boys to put up with listening to stories about girls all the time, but we do expect girls do it.'

One would hope that there has been sufficient attention to the gender bias in the traditional choice of English classroom readers to make this less typical of English teaching in general. However, the following 'mock' reading list was compiled from a quick survey of representative class readers used with 11-year-olds and still retains some element of truth.

Secondary school reading list

Pupil [in a child's voice, beginning excitedly, gradually becoming disillusioned]:
   The Magician's Nephew
   Old Mali and the Boy
   The Boy who was Afraid

Joby
Treasure Island [*Pre-20th. century*]
Buddy
Danny, Champion of the World
Goalkeeper's Revenge
Conrad, the Factory Made Boy
The Machine Gunners
I am David
Teacher [resignedly]:
Your daughter doesn't seem to enjoy reading, Mrs Smith.

In the middle years, where the reading of fiction is largely a question of voluntary reading and personal choice, the divergent tastes of boys and girls are reinforced rather than thrown into question. Sometimes reading itself can be caricatured as a girl-preferred activity. One boy interviewed in the survey only lightly veiled his contempt for the books he knew the girls in his class choose to read. When asked to talk about the 'good readers' in his group he mentioned immediately the girls who sit next to him who are

'a bit clever [*pulls a face*]. They read Judy Blume books and that and soppy things that I hate like *Forever*, and all that. It's about a girl and a boy. I don't like that either. My mum does. I read tougher books that you can really get into. Things that happen. Their books have got romance and all that and I don't like that.'

In the other gender camp, the girls frequently mentioned that boys found it harder to concentrate in private reading time and seemed less interested in reading, a tendency confirmed by the boy who said:

'If it was silent reading and if you look up across a book, you can see people that aren't concentrating on their book. Some people are looking around everywhere and you can see what's going on around you. I'm in between, like. I read a few pages then I look around. I can't really get too roped into a book.'

It was more often girls who conscientiously recorded in their reading diaries the names of authors who would feature in teacher's checklists of fiction as being most appropriate for the age range, such as Joan Aitken, Margaret Mahy and Betsy Byars. Boys' preferences included many books from the role play and fantasy adventure games genre as well as comics, computer magazines and more adult writers like Stephen King and James Herbert. Boys mentioned more often that they shared information with each other, checking facts and figures, particularly when involved in project work. They often praised books for being true, making special mention of autobiographical accounts like Roald Dahl's *Solo* and *Boy*.

Despite the efforts of teachers to accommodate boys' interests by choosing books with their tastes and resistances in mind, boys' attitudes to reading, particularly fiction, are less positive than those of girls of the same age at every stage in the education process.

Whitehead's (1977) survey of reading tastes found that:

At all ages girls read more books than boys, and at the same time there are fewer non-book readers among the girls than among the boys. Even when we hold 'ability and attainment' constant, girls of a given ability group tend to read more than boys of the same group, so that there is clearly some factor other than ability involved.

APU surveys of children's attitudes to reading undertaken in 1983 uncovered similar differences between boys' and girls' voluntary reading. Significant numbers of boys, given the choice, preferred to read non-fiction whilst twice as many girls as boys expressed a preference for reading in order to understand their own and other people's problems.

These patterns were clearly observable in the attitudes of the children interviewed in the survey. Girls frequently mentioned sharing stories with friends and swapping books with each other. They read in each other's company for long periods of time and shared reading when they stayed at each other's houses, an activity that was never mentioned by the boys. Girls also mentioned sharing books with their mothers and sisters as well as their friends. When boys mentioned reading with their mothers it was to practise their reading rather than to share a common interest in story. No one described reading with their father and only one girl had a book that she had chosen because her father had been reading it. This was Mario Puzzi's *The Godfather*.

In one of the schools in the survey the Y6 children collated a personal folder to document their achievements in the final year of their primary school. In this file they all included a photocopy of a passage of a book which they had read out aloud to either a teacher or fellow pupil to show their reading ability and interests. It was accompanied by a statement of their achievement in reading. At random I selected examples of four boys' and four girls' choices, in order to compare the passages that had been selected with the sort of reading interests expressed by their peer group in the interviews. I found that the choices they made from a common selection of books reflected the same kind of gender bias that is catered for in the comics and magazines analysed later.

Rachel had selected a passage from *Tracy Beaker*, by Jacqueline Wilson, in which the central character confides to her friend the hardship of being constantly in and out of care. Anthea had selected a passage from *This House is Haunted*, whose author she had not included in her record, in which a group of children try to find something out about the mysterious young girl they have recently met. Penny's choice was a passage from Enid Blyton that described the cute behaviour of some small rabbits and Joanne had picked a section from *Gobbolino, the Witch's Cat*, by Ursula Moray Williams describing 'what a terrible thing' it was for a small kitten to be left alone and his resolve to set out in the world to find a happy home. Each of the four passages which the girls chose to read dealt with personal feelings and relationships. In contrast, the boys' choices all reflected an interest in action and adventure.

Michael had chosen a passage from *The Computer Cheat*, by Ann Ruffu in which a boy is described as monopolizing a computer to do his homework, and Andrew had chosen *Dodos are Forever*, by Dick King Smith, which describes the destructive aftermath of a typhoon in humorous fashion. Julian's choice was a passage from *Robin of Sherwood* where the hero 'tickles' Sir Guy of Gisborne under the chin with a sword drawn from the knight's own scabbard. Martin's passage from *Star Trek*, by J.M. Dillard, described the crew being shown a replacement for the Star Ship Enterprise, a passage which had overtones of some hidden danger.

My survey of the age groups' interests in magazines and comics revealed a similar dichotomy in reading choice. Many more boys than girls read publications connected with a hobby or leisure interest, like *Angling Times* or computer magazines with facts and information, and comics that included action-packed adventures. The girls chose magazines about pop music and fashion which contained far more narrative material and personal interest stories. A closer analysis of the kinds of comics and magazines available for young readers of both sexes is very useful in highlighting the differences in language and style which exist alongside the differences in content.

Catering for the very youngest readers in the middle years age group is *My Little Pony*, a comic aimed at children slightly younger than those interviewed in my survey. Most Y6 would not admit to reading this comic though a survey of readers' letters reveal a large number of contributions from 10- and 11-year olds. *My Little Pony*'s storylines are linear and the sentence, syntax and vocabulary simple. Each tale has the same base as the sugary fantasy worlds created by some of Enid Blyton's younger texts and included in her *Sunny Stories* (*The Faraway Tree* was cited as a favourite book by several of the girls) and the characters consist of the following: the eponymous multi-coloured ponies, particularly 'baby ponies'; an assortment of 'nasty' enchantresses; potato people, glo-worms [*sic*], mermaids and witches, a dragon and a friendly giant. The most challenging words used in the publication are 'jewellery', 'scissors', 'necklace' and 'bracelets', which all occur in a 'make a necklace from coloured straws' feature. Another activity asks the readers to cut out party dresses for a rather shapeless glow-worm! Most of the stories involve eating (picnics and parties abound) and behaving well: 'The ponies tried not to giggle because they remembered what Lady lessons had told them' or helping others, 'Smasher thanked the glo-friends for rescuing him'. In the edition I am considering, a blow for girls' rights is struck by the inclusion of a story in which a girl footballer scores a goal against a male team. Her achievement however turns out to be only by accident, as the ball strikes a tree before going into the goal. 'Who says girls can't play football?' is the catch line, implying that there is more good luck than good management or skill in the girl's victory.

In sharp contrast is the publication *Thunderbirds*, whose readership, to judge by its readers' page (called Agent's Report) is a little younger. One is however, immediately struck by the greater complexity of the comic format. Frames break into each other irregularly so that the storyline seems dynamic and requires quick-witted interpretation. Whereas the *Pony* stories were narrated by a third person in the simple past tense, these rely on dialogue to carry almost all the information except for brief banner headings creating place, 'On Tracy Island' or continuity, 'Emergency Call and from Tracy Island Thunderbirds are Go!' All the written information is given in capitals. Vocabulary reflects an interest in a more material and technological world than *Pony* land. It contains phrases such as Ultra H5 guidance systems, automatic camera detectors, a marine production farm and radioactive material. Storylines include planned sabotage with 'enough explosives to destroy a small country . . . fused and timed to explode in two and a half hours loose on the high seas' and the exploitation of peasant islanders: 'But even in an island of great wealth there are those who exist on the borders of starvation. Misery and despair seem to hang in the air.' The feature article gives technical data on a Gray and Houseman Road Builder, using a numbered data plan to show exact mechanical details. There is also a competition to win a Thunderbirds' Walkie Talkie: 'All you have to do is tell us how many times the word Thunderbirds appears on this page' (an excellent exercise in scanning for specific detail). The reading positions afforded by these varied formats are challenging and offer reading practice in many forms other than narrative.

At the more sophisticated end of this age range, similar comparisons can be made between girl-directed and boy-directed magazines. The two I have chosen to analyse are *Shoot* and *Big*, both of which feature in the leisure reading of the older pupils interviewed. Although *Shoot* concerns itself obsessively with the game of football, it presents information in a varied and challenging way, mimicking journalism with its punning headlines, such as 'The Blues Brothers are back on Song' which turns out to be about two footballers who have been injured for a while and are now beginning to play well again and 'Tyne and Cheer', a story of Newcastle's success in the football league.

The girls' favourite magazine choice, *Big*, also employs a lively format with a wide range of headings, font styles, inserts and photographs, but almost all the articles concern themselves with accounts of the personal tastes, lifestyles and emotions of pop stars and personalities, told in a chatty narrative style. For example an article about Betty Boo has the same concerns and simple prose style as a *My Little Pony* story. The latter has a story called *Silver Shoes and Shabby Slippers.* which begins

> Dancing Butterflies [a pony's name] was practising her butterfly ballet when she saw little Princess Fiona in the grass below. Prince Merrin chooses a bride tonight. She must be a graceful dancer.

The Betty Boo article reads:

> Betty isn't talking today. She looks cold, tired and very thin as she arrives for the *Big* photo shoot. She is wearing black leggings, a black tee-shirt and not a scrap of make-up on her face.

Each story in its own way is about the same preoccupation with appearance and performance. Both comics and the magazines reinforce the view that men act, that is they score goals, get fit, win matches, whilst what is all important to the girls is their personal appearance, as they have their hair done, make jewellery to decorate themselves and dance gracefully. It is easy to dismiss both the boys' and girls' leisure reading as trivial and merely a distraction from the serious task of working with continuous prose, but a closer scrutiny of sample texts directed at the age group reveal that they make quite divergent demands on their readers' general competence.

The boys' choice of reading contains fact files, league charts, puzzles to solve and a range of facts and figures about longest throws, leading scorers, hardest shots. The format is lively and invites skimming and scanning for items of interest rather than concentrating on a chronological progression. The reading skills involved are relevant to instruction manuals and newspapers rather than long narrative texts. Although the prose style is relatively simple and the syntax undemanding. Janet White's (1990) observations about the effects of boys' voluntary reading seem very pertinent:

> Boys of primary school age and beyond are practising reading on texts which are distinguished not simply by their themes of violence and terror, but also by their complex visual formats in which explosive actions interrupt the linearity of narrative sequence, and stylised representations of sound effects engage a more sensory, if less reflective, reading than is the case with classical descriptive narration.

The girls' reading matter, on the other hand, emphasizes simple chronological narration, with some speculation about the character and psyche of a range of characters both real and imaginary. Many of them enjoy stories which fit into the 'romance' theme and deal with relationships between the sexes. As recent studies have shown, 'they regard the books as instruction manuals sweetened with melodramatic suspense and sensation' (Willinsky and Hunniford, 1993: 96).

Two classroom studies of adolescents' reading provide supporting evidence that the differences in the reading preferences of boys and girls, which are a recurrent feature of my survey, have become fairly rigid by the last stage of their education. Charles Sarland (1990: 183–97) describes how, when studying his older pupils' responses to popular texts, he was unable to follow up the responses to Lena Kennedy's *Maggie* (a book chosen by a group of 15-year-old girls in a Y10 class) because all the boys refused to read it. The book the girls chose tells the story of a woman's life, from childhood to grandmotherhood, tracing her relationship with a drunkard husband in the manner of popular romance fiction. All the boys who vetoed its reading, did so after a mere cursory glance. The girls read the book on their own but Sarland, as researcher, did not record their responses in his study because he found the girls not very forthcoming. On the other hand, girls' responses to disturbing scenes in James

Herbert's *The Fog*, the book chosen by the boys, are given in detail although these express a mixture of disgust and incredulous laughter. Sarland's study re-enacts the ghettoizing of girls' reading by his acceptance that the novel they chose has an 'implied female reader', whereas all the boys' choices, including *First Blood*, a movie rather than a novel, are described as 'plural texts', open to multiple readings, even if the girls' responses to them are recorded as divergent.

Second, Gemma Moss (1989: 108–9) has described finding in the coursework assignments of her older secondary pupils, evidence that they are reworking popular fictions encountered in their private reading. She contrasts the work of two Y10 pupils, Steve and Julie, analysing both stories in terms of the genre knowledge that shapes them Moss concludes that the choice of genre reflected in the writing is gender-specific.

Steve writes a story based on a chase in which skinheads in a car pursue the narrator who is on a motor bike. He escapes to see his tormentors burst into flames under the wheels of an articulated lorry. Julie's story is called *At the Party* and is about Lisa, who, after carefully selecting an interesting outfit, goes to a party where she meets a boy whom she has 'fancied for ages'. Gemma Moss comments, 'Who the boy is, is unimportant. He simply acts as a focal point for Lisa's feelings. We don't need to know anything else about him.' She also points out that in their writing both sexes rely on specific popular genre models to create their own fictions:

> . . . the adventure story, encompassing retributive violence dealt out by the good guys to the bad, is a familiar theme in comics aimed at boys. The romance in which the girl pursues and gets her man is a familiar theme in magazines aimed at girls. From my own classroom observation I would say that teenage boys frequently take up the adventure theme in their writing, teenage girls the romance, but that it is rare for girls to write adventure stories centring round male heroes battling against innumerable odds and practically unheard of for boys to write romances.

Moss, however, challenges the most commonly held viewpoint of feminists that these gender-specific, fictional models are damaging because they result in the girls' passive acceptance of stereotypical roles. Rather, she suggests they allow a space in which gender identity can be explored, tensions between masculinity and femininity interrogated and new meanings evolved. What she does suggest is that teachers' emphasis on the content of writing as a reflection of pupils' *real* experience is irrelevant because it is impossible to separate out the conventions for representing reality in this way. Instead, she suggests that it is important to look at the models of writing offered by the fiction presented in class, concentrating on revealing to the young writers the conventions and forms which support particular plots and styles of representation.

The importance to my argument about reading in the middle years of these two studies of older pupils' written responses is that both of them support my survey's findings that, in their voluntary reading, boys and girls choose to go on very different journeys of discovery and cross each other's tracks very rarely. Moreover, the books they choose frequently serve to reinforce gender limitations, rather than lead either sex to question their tastes or opinions. Boys are more likely to be accustomed to dealing with fact and information in computer and hobby magazines or violence and complex plotting in detective and horror stories. Many boys prefer their narratives in televisual or film form, where the action becomes even more central (most of the comments that Sarland recorded are about the film versions of the texts they chose). Left to their own devices, girls settle for romance or realist fictional texts, where they become ever more sophisticated at understanding thoughts and feelings and empathizing with others' problems. On one level this has an advantage for them; more girls choose to study English Literature at 'A' level and beyond, and as adults, they continue to buy and read more fiction than men. It was Virginia Woolf who pointed out that the novel *per se* is a 'female' genre and was open to nineteenth century women writers because the author requires little experience of life outside its domestic sphere in her explorations of character, motivation and feeling. However, as Martin (1989: 59) recently pointed out, narrative is not the kind of writing that carries most authority in our culture so that girls 'are being depowered from the very first stages of literacy'.

Moreover, girls' reading appears to be exactly that – reading that is confined to the girls – whereas boys' choice of reading assumes the place of the dominant mode, able to exercise universal appeal, particularly in its adult literary form which attracts a largely male audience, while allowing space for women's deconstructive readings. The point is that the books boys choose are assumed to have more interest for girls than vice versa and teachers often reinforce this by taking their choices and opinions more seriously than those of the girls just as Sarland has in his study. At the heart of the problem is the emphasis on the personal nature of response to reading, coupled with an insistence on the pleasure element which has led teachers to encourage pupils to pursue their own interests in fiction, rather than taking a more pro-active role in directing their choice or encouraging certain kinds of response.

The trend in the years following the publication of Margaret Meek's *The Cool Web* which included James Britton's strong arguments against the too early introduction of literary critical approaches to reading (Britton, 1977: 106), has been towards an emphasis on the role of the teacher in promoting reading rather than as the teacher of specific works of literature, so that teachers have been occupied with book promotion and the encouragement of reading for leisure. This had the effect in the mid-1970s of encouraging the development of excellent educational library support services, school bookshops, writers in schools projects, and also saw a rapid increase in the publication of a wider selection of attractive new titles in the teenage book market. There is however in Britton's essay, an accompanying acknowledgement that children's responses to story form depend on a 'legacy of past satisfactions'. In allowing pupils to select only books that confirm their existing tastes and interests, these past satisfactions may build on a very limited and limiting focus that works directly against a policy that promotes equal access to the curriculum.

Research has begun to concentrate in detail on the nature of pupils' response to literature (Hayhoe and Parker, 1990; Stibbs, 1991). Mick Connell has argued that 'reading for enjoyment' is a description appropriate only to lower levels of effort in the task of making meaning from texts and is misleading when used to describe the most demanding kinds of reading teachers would like pupils to undertake. Unfortunately it is the 'pleasure' element that has been most commonly emphasized in the promotion of reading in school. Work on fiction in class, both in late junior school and early in the secondary phase, has emphasized enjoyment through book reviews, reading logs and comment books. Similarly, class readers have been used as a jumping-off point for work that moves away from the text rather than closer scrutiny of it. This is particularly true of the junior phase of education, where a story read in class is often the stimulus for a project incorporating objectives from the Science or Humanities National Curriculum targets rather than a subject for study in its own right. Connell (1985) suggests that:

> the new found role of promoter of reading has increasingly become a ready and easy substitute for the more difficult and challenging role suggested by 'teacher' of literature.

The difficulty with the label, 'teacher of literature', is that immediately sends experts scurrying to select appropriate texts, reflecting the great works of English Literature for assessment purposes. In fact, what Connell intends by the description is not a return to the cold and evaluative comment encouraged by examinations, but the use of more methods which encourage close reading as well as wide reading. Children need to be given ways of working which allow them to move back into the meaning of the text in depth, a process Connell describes as 'burrowing', rather than using story only as a jumping-off point for other kinds of activities.

I have shown earlier how a close analysis of the kind of understanding expected of their readers by the magazines and comics produced for the junior age range reveals a marked contrast in their use of varied formats and specialist vocabularies. It is still a commonplace in education to emphasize the superiority of girls' reading achievement at school mirrored in their greater success in English examinations at 16, although very little serious attention seems to have been given to ways of redressing the imbalance. Certainly in their early writing, many girls draw more confidently on a range of narrative structures and are able to develop character and setting more effectively. It is also, however, equally possible to see the girls' reading experience as being too narrowly restricted by their very rapid adaptation to the story-based nature of most of their early reading. Understanding and empathizing with character, motivation and feeling is an excellent preparation for literary studies or work in the caring professions, but it may not be quite so good an introduction to studying more dense texts with technical information which requires grasping quickly. The reading that boys select for themselves includes far more information and non-narrative material than that chosen by girls. In one West Midlands comprehensive school an advisory teacher, working on reading for information, took a large selection of non-fiction texts into a group of Y7s and described how the boys fell on the selection, showing off the good bits of information to one other, whilst the girls preferred to keep to fiction. She concluded that the girls only chose to read non-fiction books when they were specifically seeking information and had been given a specific task the boys were used to collecting bits of information and had a wider interest in it. Not only is reading for information less likely to be part of a girls' voluntary activity, in the early years of secondary school very little opportunity may be provided for dealing with complex information texts in any subject.

This is an important consideration for English teachers at the beginning of secondary schooling. The evidence from the follow-up interviews in the secondary schools is that curriculum organization for the older age range has a tendency to discourage the wider reference reading encouraged by the best of primary topic work. Whereas many of the boys in the class will still follow up interests by choosing non-fiction for their library books, and choosing to read specialist journals and magazines in keeping up with hobbies, many girls continue to choose only narratives for their personal reading. In my follow-up survey of the pupils in their first year of secondary schooling, only one of the girls reported having borrowed a work of non-fiction from the school library. Helen, one of the most widely read pupils I interviewed, reported recently borrowing books on the care of small mammals to help solve her hamster's recurrent illnesses. Christine, expressed in her second interview an interest in reading information but admitted borrowing only fiction and autobiographies from both the school and local libraries. The problem for her was that in the subject structure of her new curriculum all the information she was asked to use was contained in her class texts. This is her response to the question of whether she ever borrowed books to find out information in other subject areas:

'No, you see we have class books that are for certain subjects so we don't. We have a big history book, which we read if we want any information, so we don't like go down to the school library to find out information, it's just all in that book that we're doing for that certain topic.'

She suggests that she misses the topic work that was part of learning in her primary school:

'We had one topic for the whole class – 'cos the last year we were doing fire, OK? And the teacher would give us certain groups, like we were in twos or threes, and we had to find out this bit of information. Sometimes we had to draw pictures and find out what we could about the thing. And sometimes she'd give us a topic, like – Romans, we had to do about Romans and how they dealt with fires and how the Romans used fire. Somebody would be doing how they used

fire and somebody would be doing how they dealt with fires and so that was good
when we had to share our ideas . . . she'd just tell us what we had to do and then
we'd go to the library . . .

Christine thinks it is the secondary school curriculum that compartmentalizes
her learning:

'You see here we have more topics and it would be a bit hard if all the teachers
were giving us topics to go to the library because we'd have a pile of books.
Maybe it's easier when we have just class books.'

The current emphasis on the importance of individual subjects within the
National Curriculum at the junior level may very well reduce opportunities for
such wide-ranging interests in the earlier age group. Matthew, in his primary
school interview, had discussed the difficulty of determining the relative value
of different sources of information and had explained how he had checked
some of the details or his golfing project with other boys in his friendship
group. When I met him again in his first term of his secondary school and
asked him about his reading he said that he hadn't had to do much because: 'I
haven't really started any topics. In history there's text books you have to read,
in science there's worksheets, and geography we've got these red booklets.'
These were information booklets produced by his teacher. He thought it was
because they had not been given any specific research to complete and that the
information was already sorted out and organized for them by the subject
teacher.

The dilemma for the English teacher working in such a context is whether
to take on the problem of reading for information during English time or to
work alongside colleagues to ensure that they provide opportunity for carefully
researched information in their own subjects. Schools who have tried to make
library work more central to the younger secondary age range frequently chose
to do this on a library skills basis, using arbitrary topics chosen for the simulation
of real research purposes rather than integrating the use of the library into
specific work in curriculum areas. In one comprehensive school where I was
interviewing children in the school library, about their reading interests, I
observed one such lesson where the class were given specific topics to research.
The tasks chosen for boys included football, fishing and cars while the girls
were given research topics which included the Royal Family, recipes and
animals.

Another response of many specialist English teachers to encouraging research reading is to allow pupils a choice of their own projects. During observations of a large number of Y7 and Y8 classes on-teaching practice I have
frequently drawn students' attention to the way many children fall back on
primary school topics when given an information-based topic to complete. One
of the most popular ways of introducing research topics was to ask Y8 pupils
to present information about their hobbies to other members of the class.
Many pupils brought in the work they had completed in their last two years in

primary school and added only a minimum of new information. Among the girls, topics were often very limited in scope concentrating on pop groups, pets and aspects of the fashion industry. Boys on the whole had wider-ranging taste including football, angling, model making and computer science, but many of these could be researched from the specialist magazines that they bought rather than by choosing books from the school or local library, and in many cases the wide range of interests was illusory as an individual pupil might tackle the same topic each time he was asked to work on a project.

The resulting work can look very much like the now frequently quoted, cynical method of completing a term's topic explained to a new pupil by Victor, a character in Jan Mark's *Thunder and Lightnings*:

> 'I do fish every time. Fish are easy, they are all the same shape.'
> 'No they're not,' said Andrew.
> 'They are when I do them,' said Victor. He spun his book round with one finger to show Andrew the drawings. His fish were not only all the same shape, they were all the same shape as slugs. Underneath each shape was a printed heading: BRAEM; TENSH; CARP; STIKLBAK; SHARK. It was the only way of telling them apart. The shark and the bream were identical, except that the shark had a row of teeth like tank traps. 'Isn't there a 'c' in stickleback?' said Andrew. Victor looked at his work. 'You're right.' He crossed out both 'k's, substituted 'c's and pushed the book away, the better to study it. 'I got that wrong last year.'

Victor's cynicism has been induced by a task that has no real relevance for the learner and therefore produces no new learning. Self-directed research also carries with it the gender limitations that are shaped by interest and experience. Like Victor, boys choose to write about hobbies such as angling and interests like football; girls research horses, dancing and, if their teachers permit, pop groups.

Reading for information for this age group does not have to be like this as is evidenced by the kind of work achieved in the last years of primary school in topic work grounded firmly in the curriculum. Where children had kept a file of records of their achievements in reading and writing selected by themselves, I found that both boys and girls had undertaken a much wider range of research topics. It was possible to infer common themes and project topics which had informed all the pupils' work but unlike their records of reading these did not divide so rigidly on gender lines. The work that term had included a study of the properties of water and wood in Science and a project on writing for newspapers. But what stood out just as clearly was the way in which each pupil had been allowed to pursue different aspects of each topic and to present the ideas researched in a variety of formats.

Joanne had chosen to include her study of waterfowl, the uses of wood and an account of an individual project to plant a cherry tree in the school grounds. Rachel included work on constructing a wormery, a newspaper article on wasp stings, a study of the growth of an onion, and a detailed botanical study of a piece of grass from the school playing field, as well as an account of an experiment to show water pressure. Anthea had included a study of how wood was used to make furniture, a description of the construction of a waterwheel, and a researched article on the origins customs associated with St Valentine.

Andrew had written about different kinds and qualities of wood, an account of the construction of a waterwheel and an interview for the newspaper with older children about youth clubs. Julian, had included a description of the uses of a hammer, completed a history of wooden ships, a newspaper article on basketball and his correspondence with the retired football manager, Brian Clough. Martin's work had a beautiful set of diagrams of tools, a comparison of two wading birds with illustrations composed on the computer using an art package and accounts of experiments with water.

In presenting their work in a range of formats the class were also able to show their familiarity with different genres and explore a variety of ways of conveying information. Whereas in their selections of fiction, these boys and girls had chosen very different themes and genres, according to gender interests, in their information gathering there were fewer observable differences of content choice. The most obvious ones were in their contributions to a class newspaper, where the boys had given much more emphasis to sport and hobbies. Because their choices for research had grown out of the curriculum and the reading they had undertaken was shaped by a real need to find relevant information, they had not been influenced so much by their current personal preoccupations. The emphasis on working from interest and committed research is central to their class teachers' view of the learning process. However, rather than starting from what the class already considered to be of importance, he believed that it was his responsibility to determine the overall structure of learning while working to create learning situations over which pupils could exercise personal choice.

'What I think is, you know, the National Curriculum, it's just too broad, it doesn't leave anybody with the freedom to go and do something, who knows something about it to do it really well and really beautifully and for children to learn an awful lot in a really good way about something specific. Because I believe that they do it well, it doesn't matter what you do, if I transfer those skills into anything else. I believe that if I'm doing something really well on databases, I know there's a rather tenuous link I always try to make with the writing, but I mean, I believe that, that if they've been through that process, you know, sort of challenging bits of information and looking at it really carefully and making assumptions about it and interpreting it, and thinking analytically about it – if they've gone through that process with that data, no matter what it was, no matter where it came from – when they're in a similar situation where they're presented with other evidence, no matter whether it's pure data or whether it's something else, they can deal with it. I don't know whether that counts as reading or not, but they're certainly getting information through interaction with text.'

The key to this particular class's skill in handling information and research is the teacher's enthusiasm for the projects undertaken and a willingness to share his enthusiasm and interest with them. He does not choose as central the pre-occupations of the age group, but these are drawn on to support the learning, as for example Julian's letters to Brian Clough which were part of the project work on newspapers.

Whereas most teachers of the junior age range instinctively feel it is accept-able, even an essential part of their role, to determine what information chil-dren should learn and make judgements about which information books to use, and how to negotiate topicwork when they present fiction, they are more likely to allow the children to follow their own interests, even when these interests are very narrowly based. This is a direct consequence of the emphasis placed on reading for pleasure, where in order to hook children on books, teachers work with the most popular interests. As I have discussed previously, this can lead in the final stages of schooling to a whole class studying the horror stories of Stephen King and their teacher arguing for the narrative complexity of what is fairly shoddy material. I am not arguing that teachers should cease to pro-mote voluntary reading in their classes or that they should not emphasize the importance of reading for pleasure, neither am I advocating the return set books with all the limitations that brings. However, it seems to me essential that all teachers of children in the middle years should have a grasp of the kinds of reading that challenge children's understanding and take responsibility for introducing them to structured learning experiences based on narrative.

This becomes of increasing importance when we understand that the free choices we offer pupils in class frequently serve to limit them to the kinds of books that confirm, rather than help them to question the conventional roles ascribed them by their gender. What is immediately pleasurable often becomes an endless repetition of the already read or a repeated practice of ideas presented within a particular genre. I recall at eleven being trapped in a series of books that purported to give an insight into the world of work. They had titles like *Sue Barton, District Nurse*, and *Amelia Livingstone, Almoner*. They seemed then to offer an infinite choice of possible careers to an aspiring schoolgirl who was unable to see that they were based on an idea that only certain professions were open to women. I cannot recall all the jobs they covered but what I am sure of is that there were no Queen's Counsel, pilots or neurosurgeons, as options in their formulaic representations of adult women's lives.

The response from teachers to reading matter that they consider limiting and limited should not be a blanket ban, nor even one of overt disapproval. Rather, options offered to readers by popular culture, both as textual and visual narrative, need to be interrogated, not passively consumed, so that the repeated themes and limiting stereotypes can eventually be recognized.

In the second part of the book I want to examine how a particular group of teachers, who had been committed to promoting reading for a considerable period of time re-examined their curriculum to address these concerns in order to encourage their classes to take a more critical view of their personal reading and expand the range of the books their classes encountered before transferring to secondary school.

Implications for the reading curriculum

1 Teachers need to be aware of the differences in boys' and girls' reading habits and interests so that they can provide a range of activities that give all pupils experience of a wide range of genre and formats. In particular they should be aware that much of the information girls choose to read themselves is in narrative form, whereas boys read fewer works of fiction, particularly the kind of stories that explore feelings.

2 Writers require appropriate models to follow when they are composing narratives if they are to avoid repetitive use of the genres of popular culture with which they are most familiar.

3 Popular culture has a direct influence on children's understanding and is a legitimate area of study in its own right. Teachers need to be familiar with the popular forms of narrative current in their classes and provide opportunities for discussing its impact.

4 All children need to discuss their personal preferences with each other and interested adults and teachers need to be skilled in recommending appropriate books that will broaden children's tastes. Both teachers and pupils should keep records that reflect the breadth of children's individual reading interests as well as recording their tastes in fiction.

5 Non-fiction should be included in the reading curriculum of all children.

6 Teachers have an important role to play in shaping children's reading and need to choose whole-class readers that not only reflect a wide range of interests but also challenge children's understanding of cultural norms. Books with particular forms of bias, for example the totally male world offered in Tolkien's *The Hobbit*, can be read to highlight a particular omission or emphasis in the writing rather than omitted from the reading curriculum. The aim should be to provide an overall balance rather than identify a correctness of orientation in each book selected.

PART TWO
Putting principles to work

6 Reading and writing stories together

From an early age children are learning to gain mastery over the internal rules and conventions of story patterns. They begin to recognise and anticipate the rules of the game being employed in different stories.

David Jackson, *Encounters with Books*

The desultory encounter between distracted child and randomly-chosen book is one of the many enemies of progress in reading. Children need a sense of pattern and purpose in their experience of reading in and out of school.

Henrietta Dombey, *Words and Worlds: Reading in the Early Years of School*

In the secondary phase of education, English teachers look to build on the understanding of narrative developed in the early years by children's encounters with a wide variety of ways of telling and writing stories. In previous chapters I have been concerned to demonstrate the ways which informal communities of readers work to shape the reading habits of the children in school, in a manner that is often expressed through peer group pressure. The effect of this pressure is, on the one hand, to validate those kinds of reading which frequently divide on gender lines; so for example the girls in a class may exchange books in a series like *Sweet Valley High* or of a particularly popular author like Judy Blume, while boys read and confer about computer magazines or publications connected with particular hobbies. On the other hand, as I described in Chapter 3, it can also work to influence whole classes to reject the reading habit altogether as being an interest of the 'swots' in the class, so that reading is seen as an imposition of the teachers rather than a voluntary activity of interest in itself.

Now I want to describe a unit of work devised by a particular group of Key Stage 2 teachers to build on what their children already knew about story and to encourage both shared habits of reading and an understanding of those conventions which serve to support the developing reader. I shall be considering in particular some of the more formal ways in which the school worked to accommodate the new emphasis placed by the National Curriculum on children developing effective reading strategies. These included being able to make a more considered response to their personal reading by referring to particular features in the texts and considering the quality and depth of what they read.

I had chosen to engage in developmental work with a particular school in my initial survey in which I had identified consistently positive attitudes to reading among the Y6 pupils. All the pupils interviewed talked freely about their current reading interests and were able to describe a wide range of reading activities both at home and in school. They also produced ample written evidence of having read to each other and knew how to access their own records of their personal choice in books. When discussing project work, many showed a sophisticated understanding of the relative value of information books and the importance of checking their sources. The school had already developed a particularly strong programme of reading with well-chosen picture and story books in the infant department. Their reading programme included individual interviews about reading with the children and work to support the acquisition of both written and writing vocabularies. This had the full support of the parents whose close attention to the development of their children's reading skills could be seen in their frequent use of the shared comment books in which teachers' and parents' views were given equal status and which served to monitor children's progress both at home and school.

Responding to stories

Children were used to reading to teachers, parents and each other, and a shared story was often used as the starting point for a variety of activities and language work. Quite sophisticated ideas could be explored together by the youngest classes as in these examples of work done by six- and seven-year olds who used John Burningham's *Avocado Baby* as a starting point for discussions about what boys and girls could do. The text of *Avocado Baby* is carefully constructed so that at no time is the main character given a specific gender. No gendered pronouns are used. The main character is always referred to as 'the baby' and the text itself contains no internal evidence to support the view that the baby is either a girl or a boy. Accompanying illustrations (Figures 6.1 and 6.2), however, show the baby dressed in a blue baby-grow and engaged in various feats of strength. The whole class had the story read to them and were then asked to decide whether they thought that the main character in the story was a boy or a girl. In order to make their judgements, and support their views, the children had to select relevant details from the story. They wrote independently and were asked to read their finished pieces to the rest of the group. A selection of their work is reproduced and transcribed below:

The Avocado baby is a boy becaus I think boys are strohger than girls boys do tihgs like wayt liftihg ahd thihgs like that. ahd bildihg with bricks ahd girls have longer eyelashes llas thah boys I think boys cah huh faster thah girls.

Figures 6.1 and 6.2 Y2 children's comments on the *Avocado baby*

The Avocado baby is a boy because he had shut hayre and because girls have long hayre and girls eat a lot of peas and he did not eat peas and because he can climb up trees and he lookit srong as a man

Figure 6.2

'The Avocado baby is a boy because I think boys are stronger than girls and boys do things like weight-lifting and things like building with bricks and girls have longer eyelashes than boys. I think boys can run faster than girls and boys do things like weight-lifting and things like that.'

Matthew, age 7

'He is a boy because he can break out of his cot and move furniture and lift a brick and he can break through a wall. He won't eat anything. He is a boy because he works.'

Adam, age 6

'I think he is a boy because he has to do boy's work. He picks up a car. Men are strong.'

Keiron, age 6

'I think he is a boy because he doesn't wear dresses and girls wear dresses.'

Kerry, age 7

'I think it is a boy and he can lift up a car and he can pick up six balls. He wears blue clothes.'

Louise, age 7

'The Avocado baby is a boy because he has short hair and because he did not eat peas and girls eat a lot of peas and because he can climb up trees and looks as strong as a man.'

Kirsty, age 7

Although some of their suggestions, particularly Kirsty's singular views on boys and peas, reveal how differently children's perception of what is important sometimes is, the majority of the children's comments show how well established are their notions of appropriate gender role.

The teacher was able to use the ideas expressed in their writing to help them question some of the conventional attitudes about boys and girls that they had expressed. At a very early stage these children were learning a number of complex ways of working with story. First, they were being helped to search for relevant ideas in a book to support their own interpretations of a character by using the language of the text. Second, they were discovering that stories could help to promote discussion and were enabled to use their findings to question their own first judgements. These activities were well established in working as a class with large books or multiple copies of a picture story and similar work on story was on display throughout the school.

However, in reviewing the requirements of the National Curriculum for the second stage (7–11-year olds) the language post-holder in the school felt that the work in the junior department on reading in general, and story in particular, did not build sufficiently on these early starting points. Individual reading was well established, but when pupils were asked to make their own comments on the books they were reading they lacked a shared vocabulary with which to express their views. If asked to review a book their comments were limited to simple expressions of approval or disapproval accompanied by summaries of the story.

The National Curriculum makes very specific demands at this stage for children to be able to demonstrate a quite sophisticated knowledge of story, not only in talking about the books they are reading but also in asking them to produce written stories of an appropriate complexity and development. The Reading Attainment Target asks for evidence of children's ability not only to 'read aloud unfamiliar texts expressively and fluently' but also 'be encouraged to respond imaginatively to the plot, characters, ideas and language in literature'. Similarly the Writing Attainment Target, asks for very specific narrative skills (DFE, 1993):

> Pupils should be taught to consider the effectiveness of their writing and how it can be improved, e.g. by reading their work out loud to see whether it reads well and maintains interest, and understanding when ideas are unclear or poorly expressed, where characters or descriptions could usefully be developed, or how events could be outlined more clearly.

In discussion with the other teachers of junior classes it was agreed that, although children were encouraged to read more complex fiction and to write more sustained stories at this stage in their learning, none of their current teaching practices offered direct learning experiences to develop concepts about the way we read different kinds of text. Reading was left to personal development through individual choice negotiated between pupil and teacher. Many of the children interviewed could not give any clear account of how they knew their reading was developing except to cite the number of pages they could manage, or how small the print was in the books they chose. It was clear that children needed to become more reflective about their reading so that they could make more analytical comments and judgements about the poems and stories they read, to meet the requirements for assessment at the end of the junior phase. The teachers therefore needed not only to consider the children's personal response to, and assessment of, the books they chose but to organize more opportunities for shared comment and analysis.

Group reading tasks

Often the emphasis for reading aloud in the first stage of school is on the individual reading to the teacher or another adult (Nottinghamshire Advisory and Inspection Service and Educational Psychology Service, 1991). The former activity was frequently seen by the children as a rushed and unrewarding experience. Children in the survey reported being asked to read to the next staple or to the bottom of the page without any concern on the listener's part for continuity of the story or the meaning of the passage. They reported enjoying more times when they read to a younger listener who was interested in the story rather than an adult who was 'testing' their ability. The teachers involved in the project wanted to develop a range of group reading strategies which would provide more opportunities for extended reading aloud together and an emphasis on sharing their understanding of what had been read. The class involved in the development consisted of Y5 and Y6 children in the year prior to the implementation of National Curriculum requirements for ages seven to eleven. They decided that it was important to assign particular periods of time in the school week to reading rather than allowing it to be used as a fill in 'after your work is finished', as if reading was always the optional extra. They also wanted to build on their implicit understandings of how stories were shaped by allowing them to identify the key elements in stories which helped both their enjoyment and understanding. In order to do this, the shared reading of sets of books was introduced. While groups of children were reading the same book together, the teacher was able to ask them to work in a variety of ways. Sometimes, within the group, children were paired to read a section to each other and then report their responses to the whole group. Sometimes they read round the group, taking parts as the dialogue developed. Children particularly enjoyed the group reading tasks saying it made them feel more confident because the whole class was not listening and the teacher was not there to note mistakes. They were also sometimes asked to read independently, choosing a portion of the story worth sharing with others. They then returned to the group to read their selections in chronological order and to discuss how each piece fitted into the story as a whole.

On occasions the group was set specific tasks related to the way the story was written. One such task was to look for and list as many different ways the writer had introduced direct speech with words such as 'suggested', 'screamed' or 'shouted'. On another occasion they highlighted words that were connected in meaning, for example as the language that created a mysterious atmosphere in the opening of a ghost story. In this way they were practising both skimming and scanning techniques and learning to identify descriptive detail.

Choosing books and expressing a preference

During the period set aside for individualized reading, the teacher went round the class discussing with the children their personal choice of fiction and recommending new books which would widen their horizons. In these sessions the teacher could ensure that individuals were choosing appropriate books that they were keeping their reading comment books up to date with details of all the books they had read. She also used these sessions to complete their reading records using the following format as a basis for discussing with each child not only their reading interests but also their perceptions of their own reading abilities and ways of improving.

What do I think about reading?

Name

We read because

To be a good reader I need to

Out of these I can

I am best at

In reading this year I have learnt

In my reading I would like to improve

Reading record 2

I have read ☐ fiction books this year

I have read ☐ non-fiction books this year

I have read ☐ poetry books

Out of these I prefer Poetry ☐   Fiction ☐   Non-fiction ☐

These are two or three books I have really enjoyed

Titles

They were written by

Authors

My favourite author is

I read at home   I prefer reading

every night   ☐   with someone   ☐

once or twice a week   ☐   on my own   ☐

occasionally   ☐

Following the individual discussions the teacher regularly organized a whole-class reading where the children were asked to share books and recommend them to others. They were asked to summarize some of the stories they had particularly enjoyed to help them present the book to the rest of the class and recommend the story to others. They helped each other prepare these summaries by first working in pairs to identify the key elements in the stories and to work out together how to present these to the whole class. In order to give further help with this task, the group first brainstormed the features that helped them in their selection.

They identified the following key areas that influenced their choice:

---

title
author
front cover design
an interesting blurb on the cover or fly leaf
good illustrations
one of popular series

They then listed all the aspects of a book which made it attractive to the reader. The class pooled their ideas and then the teacher devised a record sheet to help them identify and record these features in the books that they had chosen to read themselves. These ideas were set out on a sheet, designed to help focus children's attention on the ways books are put together, as well as how readers respond to them.

The record included these guiding statements:

My book is called

              by

It is:
   exciting
   funny
   happy
   mysterious
   sad

has an attractive or interesting:
   author
   blurb
   cover
   illustrations
   title

has a good:
   beginning
   middle
   end

is about

has a bit I particularly liked about

has a character I really liked called

is good because I can read it

has lots of details about

The teacher became aware, as the children began to write up their individual responses to the stories they had chosen, that their comments were limited because of a lack of understanding of the differences in particular kinds of story and the different expectations that these differences set up. To begin work with the whole class on what would eventually develop into an early study of genre, they were asked to think more carefully about the differences in the books that they chose to read. At circle time an individual child would be asked to choose a favourite book from the shelves and before the choice was made the others in the class were then asked to predict what kind of book would be chosen. A variation of this task was to ask particular children to analyse their friend's reading habits by looking at the books they had recorded in their reading diaries and those currently kept in their reading wallet. The friend would then describe her partner's reading tastes and decide what sort of book might be next on the reading list.

A variety of tasks were then devised for whole-class reading sessions which focused children's attention on the kind of books they most commonly chose to read. These included:

1 Photocopying the opening of a book and asking the children to underline the evidence that shows what kind of story it is. This might include names of characters, details of the setting, descriptions of characters or groups of similar words (lexical chains).
2 Typing out the beginning and endings to a variety books of different genres and asking the children to match them up, explaining to the class their reasons for pairing particular examples.
3 Asking a particular child to choose a favourite character from a story and describing that character to the others who, in turn, have to suggest what they thought would happen to the person in the course of the book.
4 Typing the titles of a range of stories such as *The Little Dragon Falls Out, A Game of Catch, The Moon's Revenge, The Iron Man* and asking the children to guess what sort of book each might turn out to be.

Photocopying front covers was used to determine who the publishers thought would want to read the story. The children noted the different kinds of covers using cartoons, fantasy images, realistic pictures and photographs. The children were encouraged to scan the blurbs for clues to the kind of story they led the reader to expect.

Children were also asked to answer the following questions of a book assigned to them for a quick survey.

What evidence have you found to tell you what kind of book you have been given?
What will the story be about?
Will it be serious or funny?
What age of reader do you think it was meant for: a toddler, infant, junior, teenager, adult?
Was the story aimed at boys or girls or both?
Which story might you choose to read and why?

While working on these activities the children developed a simple genre category that helped them discuss narrative in more detail. They decided that their main reading included

adventure stories	ghost
school stories	fantasy
stories which were true to life	detective fiction
humour	narrative poems

They also included narrative poems in their categories because they had recently read *The Highwayman* by Alfred Noyes and discussed the story element in other poems they had shared in reading conferences.

These activities were enjoyable in themselves and involved the class in a wide range of Speaking and Listening activities which could be observed and recorded. At the same time they also helped the children to develop a more sophisticated sense of how writers create particular effects or set about raising a reader's expectations. They used a similar brainstorm to categorize the large variety of poems they had chosen and shared in group reading sessions. They decided that poems might have some of the following features.

Poems

have verses	are like songs
have rhymes	use unusual words
sometimes don't rhyme	have a chorus
show feelings	are catchy
make you laugh	have deep thoughts
have surprises	paint a picture
may tell a story	are written in lines
miss out short words like 'and/or', but are written in shapes	

These simple categories enabled the class to talk about the poems they read in shared sessions in more detail so they could, for example, say 'My favourite line in the poem is . . .' or 'I like the way the poem paints a picture of . . .' and in this way they learned to support their views by referring to specific features of a poem they had chosen, turning a simple preference into a critical judgement.

In the following year, the teacher decided to build on their ways of talking about differences in books by helping the children to create their own stories based on a variety of genre. First of all, the children were asked to think about the many different kinds of stories they had encountered. They were encouraged to bring in story books from home and work with a partner to identify the kind of story contained in both these and the books in their reading wallets. Interestingly, several of the boys chose to bring in non-fiction books. These included a book about the Napoleonic Wars, a book about the working of the body, books about cars and several computer magazines. The first discussion was to establish the differences between non-fiction and fiction books, because as the boys were swift to point out, these books did have stories in them, particularly the history texts which had stories of battles and military campaigns. When non-fiction had been set aside the class looked at the remaining fiction texts and began to work out what kinds of stories they had chosen. On this occasion their ability to see a wider range of genres was evident. Their suggestions were then written up on a large flip chart and included the following categories:

fairy tales	ghost	animal
fantasy	legends	comedy
crime	thriller	fable
space (Sci-Fi)	war	true-to-life
adventures	school	sport (mainly
narrative poems		football)

As the children worked in pairs to describe to one another the particular stories they had selected, they were asked to concentrate on finding specific evidence to support their views on the kind of story they had chosen. They were asked to talk about any of the following features:

characters that usually appear in that type of story
actions that usually appear in that type of story
feelings that usually appear in that type of story
places where the events usually take place
objects that might be involved (e.g. a shield or ring)
how the stories opened (e.g. a mysterious challenge, a surprise event)

They were then asked to choose one of the types of story they enjoyed and write an opening to share with the class in a writers' circle.

Before reading the stories out in the circle the children were encouraged to work closely with a response partner to decide how the story might be presented to the whole class. The strategies used were based on the writing process developed by Donald Graves, with the important difference that the children were given a particular kind of narrative task, rather than a total freedom of topic and style (Graves, 1983; Temple *et al.*, 1988). Conferencing was to be an essential part of the story-writing process, concentrating initially, as Graves recommends, on the 'authorial' or compositional aspects of writing, rather than 'secretarial' concerns for correctness and presentation, which are more appropriate to final drafts. The children were given simple pointers on what to look for in each other's works to help the process. It was stressed that they should begin by listening carefully to their partner's draft and make comments on the things that they liked most or found interesting; secondly they were asked to say if there was anything in the story that they wanted or needed to know more about.

When the story was shared in a larger writers' group they were then asked to decide whether the writer had placed the story in an appropriate setting, creating an atmosphere that helped the reader make predictions of what might happen: They were also asked to say if the action started at an appropriately interesting place or if there was too much irrelevant information about getting up and getting there before anything began to happen.

Working on story openings and structures

One focus for whole-class conferences was the openings of the stories. The children read these to the class while the rest were instructed to look for the evidence that would let them know which kind of story to expect. It was a very useful activity in helping also to do further work on the idea of the 'reading aloud' skills which were part of their individual reading work. By linking reading and writing in this way the children were led to experience at first hand the strategies of authorship of giving clues, building up atmosphere, working on their readers' expectations. The conferencing sessions became the central part of the learning process and its purpose was to help the writers to see how successful they were in helping their readers get into their stories. During each writing period, which lasted a whole morning, response partners were allowed to sit together in the carpeted area to share stories and make suggestions to help each other when writing became difficult. Alternatively, a writer with a major difficulty could wait to get some further advice from a teacher. In the last half hour of the session all the class gathered together to hear a particular story and formulate their advice together. In this session the teacher was able to model, through careful open questions, an appropriate response to particular problems that re-occurred in the children's work.

The following examples are taken from selected conference sessions, where the children gathered in a closed-off carpeted area to listen to some of the openings that had been written and offer suggestions for re-drafting. In the first discussion group they concentrated on deciding what kind of stories they were listening to. In a second session they were asked to decide if it was clear from the writing who the main character was and if there was enough detail to form a picture of this character and the story's setting and action.

Writing conference 1

What have you learned about your story?

Who was your story for?

What bits did they like?

What type of story did your readers think it was?

fantasy	humorous	poem
legend	ghost	sport
adventure	animal	monster
school		

or any other story type?

As the children read out their openings it became obvious that particular problems recurred in several children's writing. One of the most persistent difficulties was a tendency to muddle two or more genres and create situations which were not in keeping with the expectations created by the titles or opening paragraphs. John presented such a story to the first whole-group

Writing conference 2

Setting
Can your reader say where the story took place?

Character
Did you tell your reader enough about your character?

Dialogue
Can we tell who is talking and what the listener is thinking?

Action
What are the main events?

conference. He had written solidly all morning, without consulting the teacher or his partner to produce a story called *The Winter Ghost* (Figure 6.3), which begins:

> One dark scary night in the middle of winter when the clouds were down children were scared everywhere. They went running to their houses. This happened for four days. All the people wondered why the ghost was laughing in the clouds.
>
> There was a boy called John, he was a boy with talent. He looked in the fire and thought he saw a face. John moved back, there it was again. He moved back even more. Then something jumped out at him. He thought to himself, 'I'm out of here.'
>
> The ghost started to chase him around the house. Then the ghost caught John. John tripped on the chair leg. The ghost jumped back into the fire with Joe. His mum is called Jane. She walked in.
>
> 'Come on, John, its time for tea.'
>
> 'Oh no, where's John?'
>
> Meanwhile the ghost and John were climbing up the chimney.

John opens his story appropriately with a spooky setting and a glimpse of a mischievous ghost face first in the clouds and then in the flames of the fire which captures John, placing him in the dungeon of a medieval castle, but then the story develops into a string of episodes involving police chases and flashbacks to the distraught mother of the victim culminating in the following episode:

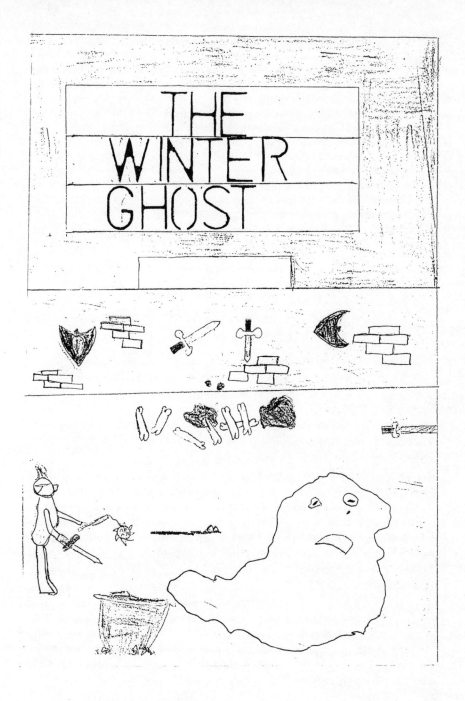

Figure 6.3 John, like other boys in his class, chose a genre that involved exciting action

The police were speeding down the road. When the ghost heard a police car he rushed out to shut the door. The police car rushed up the hill. Back in the cell, John was sitting bored. He heard the police car and said, 'Yes they're coming.'

The car was rushing up the hill as fast as it could. The police car was at the top of the hill. PC Walls, PC Cartwright, PC Harris got out of the car. PC Walls said, 'How are we going to get in because the ghost has probably locked the door?' PC Cartwright said, 'Don't worry, I've got an axe.' PC Walls said, 'Before you do that let's test the doors.'

So PC Walls tried to open the doors.

He said, 'Someone has locked the doors.' PC Cartwright started to chop down the doors. They bashed through the doors. The ghost quickly ran upstairs. PC Harrison, PC Walls and PC Cartwright ran upstairs. They surrounded the ghost.

'I've got a net.'

'Get him.'

'Yes, we've caught him.'

'Right let's get him to the van.'

Back at Jane's house, Jane was sitting watching TV. She looked at her watch. She saw it was getting a bit late.

'I'm going to bed now.'

The police set John free. He ran as quickly as he could to his mom, he knocks on the door. His mum come down and opens the door. She looks outside and sees John standing there. She puts her hands around him in relief.

'You're home at last.'

The models for John's story are half recollections of the video version of the *Ghost Busters* film which features police forces and rapid chases. The film has obviously given him the main idea for the sequences and he moves in and out of scenes as if he is following the shots of a camera and the action of a film. His story is all action and quick verbal exchanges which direct this, with no attempt to account for the characters' interactions or feelings about what is happening.

To help John think through his story more carefully the children were asked if they thought ghosts could be sorted out by the police. When they explained that the ghost had already shown it could vanish a whim and therefore would not be easily trapped in a net, they were asked how ghosts were dealt with in ghost stories. They began to describe how ghosts could be tricked into going into a bottle or container where they could be controlled. Ghosts could also be frightened away by a more powerful force or magic implement, like a sword or wand. Witches' and wizards' spells could control them. Ghosts might find something that they had hidden when they were on earth and then be content to go back from where they came. In suggesting these ideas for John's story the class were showing how much they had already learned about the way stories are structured and the rules governing particular genres. John listened to the different pieces of advice and went away to edit his story, deciding finally to alter the scene where the police catch the ghost to one where the ghost is exposed to daylight by a trick John plays on him, and in the first glints of sunlight, disappears.

Charlotte's story was called *The Magic Tree* (Figure 6.4) and was intended as an adventure but Charlotte became involved in a detailed and rather boring dialogue that prevents her from developing the action. Her characters talk too much without being provided with a context which would allow a reader to follow the story. Whereas John imagines his characters rushing from place to place in pursuit of his ghost, Charlotte eavesdrops on their conversation as she might if she were watching a TV soap, like *Neighbours*.

Here she is trying to establish the existence of a magic tree where adventures might occur.

'Do you want to know a secret, Jo?' said James.
'OK' said Jo.
'But you promise not to tell anybody . . .'
'OK, I promise,' said Jo.
'You know in the woods, well there's a magic tree there.'
'Oh no there isn't.'
'There is.'
'OK, I'll only believe you if you show me.'
'OK, tomorrow we will say to mum that we are going to play with Jim.'
'Sure,' said Jo.
'Wait,' said James, 'we could take your friend, Jim.'
'Sure, he would love to come.'
'Do your sisters know about this tree?'
'Oh no, I said it was a secret didn't I?'
. . .

and so on for two more repetitive pages before the threesome set off in search of an adventure.

The class listened a little restlessly to the story and then suggested that Charlotte needed to start her adventure much more quickly as nothing much had happened by the second page of her writing except a good deal of planning. Particular suggestions from the group included explaining how the secret was discovered and a description of the tree to arouse curiosity.

In writing their stories, John and Charlotte appear to be using models which are not text based, but shaped by their experience of narrative in other media, such as film and television. The influences that help determine their differing choices, the one focused almost entirely on action, the other on social interaction are further examples of the way gender preferences are reflected not only in children's reading, but also in their own writing.

What seemed most important from an overview of the whole group's approach to devising stories was that all the children needed to become more familiar with written rather than visual forms of narrative and the conventions that shaped their structure. One strategy was to read more short stories together and discuss how they achieved their effects; another was through role play based on some of the stories available in the class.

In their drama lessons the children were split into small groups which were all given the same three objects to work into a story which was to be acted out

Figure 6.4 Cover from Charlotte's story

for the whole class. The objects were a large piece of material to be used as they wished as a cloak, magic carpet or whatever, a lantern and a stick. The groups were given a particular kind of story to deal with selecting from adventure, comedy, ghost and fairy tales which were the genres with which they seemed most familiar.

The children acted out their devisings while the other groups tried to guess what type of story they had produced. This led to discussions about how best to create a particular atmosphere, what characters were most appropriate and how the objects could best be used. The children then used their experiences of genre to classify the kinds of books on the class shelves. They were able to transfer the knowledge gained from their group work to appreciate how a story creates certain expectations for its reader and use this in their own compositions.

Drama was also used to help children to see that stories had key incidents that were essential to plot development. The class was split into six groups of five and each group was given the title of a well-known fairy story. Although teachers may assume a knowledge of this genre among older juniors in fact many children had only vague knowledge of the key events in the stories because they muddled the originals with versions they had seen as cartoons or even advertisements. They are a particularly valuable genre because their themes reappear so often in both popular culture and more traditional literature.

Jack and the Beanstalk	The Little Mermaid
Rapunzel	Hansel and Gretel
Cinderella	The Sleeping Beauty

Each group had to decide on one or two key incidents from the story and to devise short scenes to illustrate them. After a short rehearsal, the groups were asked to freeze in role and at a command determined by calling out their group's letter, they had to recommence the action, freezing again on command.

The mini-episodes were presented in very rapid succession and then one person was asked to say if he could tell what the different stories were.

The presentations were lively and helped the class to identify key points and dramatic moments in narrative development while remembering the plots of quite complex narratives.

Endings

One group reading session had as its focus the reading of two passages that were the endings of two very different kinds of story. The children worked in small groups as 'story detectives' to work out what had taken place in the story by picking up particular clues from the text. They were therefore being asked to draw on their understanding of the significant patterns, gained implicitly from their reading and apply it to the fragments in order to reconstruct the whole. As Margaret Meek (1982) has pointed out in *Learning to Read* '[a reader] understands how the ending helps him to reconstruct the beginning.' To help the pupils in their deductions they were asked to think about the following question

---

1 Who are the main characters in the story?
2 What do you think has happened in the story so far?
3 How do you think the story started?
4 Think of a title for this story.

One text was the ending of a comic fantasy adventure story featuring Norman Hunter's Professor Branestawm, the second was a version of an American fable, written by Julius Lester.

'If only people would leave my inventions alone,' said the Professor to Mrs Flittersnoop later on, after a good strong cup of tea and strengthening scones, 'there would be no trouble. Now I shall have to write my own letters again.'

'Yes, indeed I'm sure sir,' said Mrs Flittersnoop, feeling thankful another attack of inventions was over.

Helpful notes:
What do you think the Professor's new invention might have been able to do?
Who is Mrs Flittersnoop and why do you think she is glad that it is all over?

The snake looked at the farmer and said, 'That's what I promised, but remember, Mr Farmer, I'm a snake. You knew that when you picked me up. And you know that snakes bite. It's a part of their nature.' Fortunately the farmer was close enough to town so that he could go and see the doctor and got some medicine before the snake's poison got to work on him. After that though the farmer knew. If it's in the nature of a thing to hurt you, it'll do just that, no matter how kind you are to it.
                    The Oxford Blue Story Book, Jackson and Pepper (eds)

Helpful notes:
What has happened to the farmer?
Think carefully about why the farmer might have thought it was safe to pick up the snake.

The children enjoyed searching for clues together and trying to reconstruct the stories from their endings. They quickly worked out the first story using the clues to suggest that the professor had invented a machine to write letters which had got out of control because other people had tampered with it. They could deduce that the problems had been caused by rude letters and that Mrs Flittersnoop was the person who looked after the professor. This story format was very familiar to them and they understood the way comic plots developed. Without conferring, the groups all chose either *The Writing Machine* or *The Professor Invents a Writing Machine*, as the story's title. The second task was more problematic. Even when they had worked out that the snake had bitten the man the children found it very difficult to understand why he had picked it up in the first place. Someone suggested the farmer was going to steal its skin, another that he wanted to kill it. What was evident as they discussed the story and its ending was that none of them was familiar with the idea of a fable where animals and human beings treat each other as equals. Their choice of titles however suggested that they had begun to work out some of the main ideas contained in the story. They included *The Broken Promise*, *The Crafty Snake* and *The Farmer and the Snake*.

This work was done orally with various groups meeting in the conferencing area to share their ideas or puzzle out a difficulty with the help of the teacher. At the end of the session the complete stories were read to the group and they listened carefully to discover how close their predictions had been to the actual story. After listening to the story of *The Farmer and the Snake* they decided to research other stories like this and were given the task of finding another fable before the next discussion session to read aloud to the other children. Reading out stories, whether as part of the conferencing sessions on their own writing, or as part of the group sessions discussing ideas, became an important part of the work on story.

One of the outcomes of the development work was the creation of a bank of short stories written in particular genres which afforded the teachers opportunities to discuss the shape and organization of a particular story as well as its content. Stories which the teachers agreed had made most impact on understanding were bought in small sets; others, such as versions of myths and fairy tales were kept as single copies collected together in baskets according to their genre so that when a reader selected a book from the collection they were reminded of the kinds of stories available.

The following is a list of the books which one group of junior school teachers had found most useful in the group reading sessions. Many could also be used with a whole class for more extended writing models. They include several collections of stories because these lend themselves most readily to writers' workshop activities and group reading sessions. Ideas for working with the books, particularly directed reading activities which develop understanding of plots, settings and characters, were collected as part of the school's resources. These were further supplemented with ideas from commercially produced support materials such as Macmillan's 'M' Book File (Leggett *et al.*, 1990) and *Making Stories* and *Changing Stories* (English and Media Centre 1984a and b), currently available through NATE Publications, Sheffield. All of these contain many suggestions for directed reading activities that build awareness of story structure.

Suggested titles for group reading activities

Tales of a Fourth Grade Nothing	Judy Blume
Flat Stanley	Jeff Brown
*The Eighteenth Emergency**	Betsy Byars
The Julian Stories	Ann Cameron
Dear Mr Henshaw	Beverley Cleary
Fantastic Mr Fox	Roald Dahl
Bill's New Frock	Anne Fine
Private Keep Out	Gwen Grant
*The Shrinking of Treehorn**	Florence Parry Heide
*The Iron Man**	Ted Hughes
*How the Whale Became and Other Stories**	Ted Hughes
The Flat Man	Rose Impey
Fairy Tales	Terry Jones
Comfort Herself	Geraldine Kaye
*Harry's Mad**	Dick King-Smith
*The Battle of Bubble and Squeak**	Phillipa Pearce
The Shadow Cage and other Stories	Phillipa Pearce
The Bakerloo Flea	Michael Rosen
*Clever Polly and the Stupid Wolf**	Catherine Storr
Gobbolino the Witch's Cat	Ursula Moray Williams
Dr Xargles Book of Earthlets	Jeanne Willis
The Story of Tracy Beaker	Jacqueline Wilson
There's a Wolf in My Pudding	David Henry Wilson

They included several narrative poems

The Pied Piper of Hamelin	Robert Browning
Revolting Rhymes	Roald Dahl
*The Highwayman**	Alfred Noyes
*The Listeners**	Walter de la Mare

Books in the selection that are included in the National Curriculum list of recommendations for this age group are marked with an asterisk (DFE, 1993). This does not however mean that the list is a prescriptive one. Rather it represents the choices made by a particular group of teachers.

There was also a large collection of picture story books which could be used for private reading, or as a model for writing a picture story for young children. A group of Y7 children in one of the survey schools had used a collection of picture books to analyse what was most effective in the books they enjoyed when they were younger, producing their analysis in a simple format which guided them to the key features of the text.

Reading aloud

At the time when Frank Whitehead began his enquiries into children's reading habits at the end of the 1960s and early 1970s, the private reading of children's fiction in the secondary school was an activity confined to their leisure time. Reading as an activity in the English lessons of older children was frequently focused on a set text which was read round the class 'for practice' and which provided the teacher with material for language work and a general focus for discussion. Whitehead (1966) in his recommendations therefore takes for granted that 'reading aloud' is an essential part of the pupils' experience in English lessons:

> Although the immediate goal for these pupils is to undertake silent reading effectively, it remains true that the approach to this goal must be through practice in reading aloud. The teacher is compelled to concentrate on reading aloud at this stage because only thus can 'he obtain close contact with the process of re-thinking the ideas on the printed page' which constitutes the essence of the reading act and thereby gain the power to affect and influence it.'

What was seen in 1966 as an essential part of every 11-year old's reading experience is no longer part of current practice, either at the end of the junior phase or the beginning of secondary education. Teachers frequently feel anxious about asking children to read out aloud to a whole class and allow only the most confident readers to share the task of reading a class book with them. In consequence, many children have little practice in getting the words directly from the page and are hesitant and uncertain about their reading abilities.

In describing their reading, 20 children, a fifth of the group who had completed the *Stories of Reading* questionnaire said they disliked reading out loud, 12 of whom were boys and eight girls. Only three pupils claimed to enjoy reading out loud and the rest of the children who had completed the questionnaire made no comment. This seems to confirm teachers' perceptions that reading aloud is an off-putting task which has little benefit for most pupils.

Yet, when interviewed, the older children in my study frequently stated that they missed the opportunity for sharing their reading with others in the later years of junior school. They were very tolerant of each other's hesitancy and showed an awareness of the kinds of support they could give to someone stumbling in their reading. What children disliked then was not reading out loud to each other but preforming in front of a critical adult audience where they were given little control over their choice of subject matter.

Christine's comments about reading aloud in history lessons reflect the views of many of her age group:

> 'I find it annoying when I have to listen to somebody who's stumbling but I try to be patient with them because they're not very good at reading. And sometimes the teacher tries to give people a chance to read it by themselves and sometimes their friends sitting near them will help them along, so it's OK. When they're reading, not very good readers, but the good readers get chosen to read when there are particularly hard quotes in that passage.'

Many teachers' concern not to pressurize children by enforcing reading out from class readers or their unwillingness to allow a shared story to lose momentum by being subjected to the monotonous and hesitating delivery of a slow reader, has resulted in most of the oral reading being done by teachers themselves or the children who have already proved themselves to be competent.

Children's reading in class has often been based on reading out their own compositions so that it can be commented on by the others, while the reading of fiction remains an individual or paired activity. The implications of this are that there is little opportunity for many children to practise reading carefully crafted prose with the kinds of rhythms and literary devices that make them memorable. On the other hand, the increase in availability of story tapes, read by well-known personalities has meant that most children have had a wide range of examples of good reading on which to model their own performance. Some of the group reading sessions were therefore organized around reading out aloud so that the children could be helped to identify the criteria for good oral presentations of written material.

Initially, the class was asked to think of all strategies that helped them read aloud in an interesting and enjoyable way. They came up with the following list of good ways that a reader could engage a listener's interest:

Change speed to match the content of the story
Change volume
Change voice to represent a character e.g.
    croak for the Frog Prince, boom for a giant,
    cackle for a witch
Change accent to suggest a 'posh' character or someone from a
    different area
Change pitch (the children called this making your voice high or low)

The children's practical advice to a reader included:

Look at the audience
Position the book well
Create an atmosphere by emphasizing special words and phrases
Make your tone sound angry, spooky, mysterious or humorous
Practise reading to someone else

They were asked to practise a favourite passage from their own books to read out to someone else either at home or in school. They were then asked to identify, from their *own* reading, the strategies they had employed, choosing one area they thought could be improved on. Their partner could also help them by first identifying the positive features of their reading style and then making one or two suggestions for its improvement.

The class were given a variety of opportunities to read aloud in class by presenting a favourite selection of poems in groups or acting out a section of the group reading book or by taping a book for use with younger children or by choosing to read to children in the reception class. These activities were repeated at intervals throughout the year and organized to include everyone at some time. Reading aloud provided a specific purpose for reading the passages closely and highlighting specific details. In order to keep a record of their reading aloud the children chose one of the passages they had read to a friend to be photocopied and included in their record of achievement alongside an accompanying description of how well the passage had been read.

Parental involvement and comment books

One of the cornerstones of the practice in this school was to involve parents in their children's reading development through a shared comment book in which both teacher and parent or guardian commented on the reading they had shared with the child. It seemed important for the developing reading programme that teachers should sustain this contact with the children's parents through the reading comment books begun at the infant learning to read stage. They wished to show parents that although the children were growing more independent as readers and almost all of them could read silently, they would still benefit from adult interest and needed support for their personal choices through discussing their books with adults both at home and at school. However, it seemed a waste to spend time making individual comments about a group activity in each child's book so a comment explaining carefully the work that had been done in each session was written and photocopied for each child.

25 November 1991

Your child has been practising reading aloud to get the audience interested in the book. Can you help them this week by:
* reading it out loud first so that they can hear how it could sound;
* make your voice go loud/soft/slowly etc.;
* asking them to have a go at reading it out now and look at last week's comment to see what technique they were going to try next time they read aloud.
How did you get on?

---

4 February 1992

This week we have spent time looking at different types of stories like fairy tales, animal stories, horror, ghost, mystery, adventure, etc.

We have listed the types of things that crop up regularly in each kind of story. For example fairy stories often contain wicked witches, spells being cast and talking animals; animal stories often have families in them, animals getting lost and found.

We are thinking about how the title, cover and opening of a book convey which type of story it might be.

I like choosing

stories

---

16 February 1992

This week we have read the opening to one of our books to a group of children and then everyone in the group was asked to guess what the rest of the story might be about.

We found that in some stories

---

2 March 1992

Today I recommended one of my books to the rest of the group. First they
had to guess what sort of books I liked reading from the choices in my
reading wallet.

I like

I recommend

because

In each case the child completes the last sentences. Through these photocopied
messages the teacher helped parents and other supporting adults to understand
the importance of the work being done in reading towards shifting children's
attention from reading aloud to an understanding about the way books create
meaning. These activities emphasized the importance of children being able to
choose books in an informed way while developing a vocabulary to explain the
reasons for their choice to others. Reading is given the role of a central curriculum activity rather than that of a peripheral occupation of time when other
work has been completed.

In the APU's summary of its surveys of language performance conducted in
1988 to the Schools Examination and Assessment Council (*Assessment Matters*,
no. 4: *Language for Learning*, HMSO, 1991), it was reported that secondary
pupils

> find it easier to be consumers and users rather than analysts of literary or media
> effects.

It further suggested that

> Pupils require an understanding of the distinctive features, forms and conven-
> tions of functionally different text types. Both teachers and pupils need more
> guidance recognising and exploring genre. This is an area in which the National
> Curriculum Statements of Attainment are not, however, explicit. The simple
> literary/expository distinction is not adequate to characterise the range of read-
> ing materials that pupils need to understand. Knowledge of this kind can be
> considered part of 'being literate'; it can be 'caught' by a wide exposure to a
> range of different reading materials, but it can also be taught.

In providing a variety of opportunities for the class to share their
understandings and predictions of how stories are shaped and preferences
expressed, the teacher is not only laying the foundation for the development of

more analytical work with texts in the later stages of schooling, but also showing the children that reading is a valued part of their learning process, not simply an activity that is squeezed into the gaps between other subject learning. What is being established is the habit of reflecting on reading and an ability to share these reflections with others. Children are being asked to examine their implicit judgements of what makes a good book and to find descriptions for communicating these judgements to others which also helps to inform their understanding of the conventions of writing about books. In the process, their view of reading is shown to have importance and their new understandings of how books are structured is connected to their growing control over their own story writing and development of ideas. They are becoming a part of a reading community that values the skill of creating stories and whose members are developing an effective discourse to communicate their interests and pleasure one to the other.

Margaret Meek (1992: 172–89) has recently alerted teachers, to the fact that 'as young readers become more confident we seem to spend very little time helping them to understand what writers are doing when they tell stories'. Her suggestion is to work with fiction that prods readers into questioning 'what kind of a book, what kind of a story is this?' The narrative work that these children engaged in prepared them to ask these questions both a personal and a critical way and led them to informed discussions about what they were reading with each other, their teachers and their families.

The proposals for the teaching of English for ages 5–16 years published in April 1993 give a less prominent place to narrative in the early Attainment Targets and introduce the idea of reading literature for this age group. There is a danger that without sufficient attention to the emerging understanding of how stories are shaped the study of literature will turn into the sterile quotation spotting and single sentence comprehension exercises that used to be the stock in trade of literature examinations for the older age groups. This does not have to be the case. The children whose work appears in this and the following chapter have not only read widely and independently but have also been given many opportunities to talk about books together and build shared habits of interpretation and comment. These are the firm foundations on which a personal and literary response to more complex texts can be built in the secondary English curriculum.

Conclusions

1 In order to address all the reading requirements of the National Curriculum, teachers of junior children need to use more group reading strategies and directed reading activities which help children make sense and respond to a wide range of story genre.

2 Children need to be encouraged to practise reading aloud and should be enabled to share their reading with others. More activities which involve

presentation of well-written material to others need to be programmed into the curriculum at all levels.

3 At Key Stage 2 and beyond, children need to develop a way of talking about books which goes beyond the expression of simple preference. They can be helped to do this by sharing writing and using conference sessions to determine exactly what makes a story worth reading.

4 There is a danger that National Curriculum requirements that children pick out key points in texts will herald a return to simplistic comprehension and gap-filling exercises. Other strategies can be used that help children to scan for specific ideas and details whilst working on an engaging story. These include highlighting or underlining details of character and setting and preparing passages for reading aloud.

5 Key Stage 2 teachers should begin to collect multiple copies of the books which they use as group or class readers. Banks of ideas for working with these books should form part of each school's resources for learning. There should be a collection of poetry anthologies. The teacher's own ideas can be supplemented by commercially produced resources such as Macmillan's 'M' Book File.

6 Parents have a continuing role to play in encouraging their children's wider reading and can be supported in this role through a shared comment book to which teachers, pupils and readers make contributions.

7 Making good use of information

'I've never been much of a reader to be honest. I don't enjoy reading at all because it's boring and I don't like reading out loud because I don't like reading. I only buy magazines or, as the case may be, one magazine, called *Improve Your Coarse Fishing* which hasn't got any characters in it. Most of my teachers seemed to like reading poems to people and stories about our topics.'

Russell, age 11

Russell's opinions on reading were shared by a large proportion of the boys I interviewed, particularly those from less privileged backgrounds where the reading of fiction was not, in their experience, a common part of the adult world, but something peculiar to the interests of their teachers. Russell also gets very little credit in school for the voluntary reading he really enjoys and which provides him with a range of written formats for presenting information. For Russell reading in school is something unconnected to his life outside and therefore has little relevance or importance in his scheme of things. Asked to comment on how he thinks people view his reading he says: 'Getting better, that's all they ever say and I hope they are right!' He does not, however, seem to believe that he can do anything to assist in this development; the improvement will, if he is lucky, just happen. Much teaching of reading in the middle years of schooling appears to rest on an assumption that fluency in reading narrative will lead to a parallel competence in dealing with non-narrative genres. Research, however, consistently shows that this expectation is not founded on real evidence; in fact, quite the contrary – fluent readers of narrative may experience considerable difficulty in managing information (Littlefair, 1991: 127, 129, 138).

Children need different kinds of reading skills to make the best use of the factual genres they meet in their search for information. In Chapter 4, I discussed evidence that shows boys in general read a wider variety of genres than girls and that in particular their leisure reading contains more technical information and complex, non-chronological structures than the chronological narratives that are the girls' choice. It can be argued that this earlier exposure to different ways of organizing information may explain some of the later advantages boys gain over girls in dealing with more technical, and factually based subject areas of the curriculum. It also accounts for many boys' dissatisfaction with a school reading curriculum that stresses the pleasure of reading books, which for them present nothing but a troublesome imposition. Not only this, but familiarity with narrative structures is not necessarily the best preparation for dealing with the wide range of information texts that will eventually be part of the secondary curriculum. The National Curriculum places a strong emphasis on the need for children to be able to seek out information and make use of it independently of the teacher. At Key Stage 2 they are expected to

> know how to find information in books and databases using organisational de-
> vices (chapter titles and headings, subheadings, glossaries contents and indexes)
> to help them decide which parts of the material to read closely. They should be
> taught how to read appropriately adopting appropriate strategies for the task.

At Level 1 children should already be able to 'talk in general terms about what they have found out in a non-fiction text' and At Level 3 'select specific information from a non-fiction text' (DFE, 1993).

To be effective readers of non-fiction, children will need to develop very different skills from those associated with reading narrative. The chronological structure of the former leads the child to read continuously, moving from the opening of a story to its ending in a methodical and concentrated linear path. Children in the survey judged their peers' ability to read well by their powers of concentration, their ability to read a large number of pages in a session and their refusal to skip pages, or to give up a particular book before it had been completed.

The skills needed to make good use of information texts is almost diametrically opposed to the process of concentrated absorption which is appropriate to the reading of fiction. Information books need to be quickly surveyed for their relevance to the information required, using textual structural pointers like contents pages, indexes, chapter headings and subheadings, glossaries and even the date and place of publication. Children need experience in skimming for general impressions and scanning to locate specific details in the books. These are skills which many of them begin to acquire through the information they find in their hobby and computer magazines, rather than from the books provided for them in school.

The language of most information texts is also markedly different from that found in narrative, so that not only do developing readers need to approach information books from a different angle, but they also need to become familiar with a whole new range of linguistic structures which are rarely found in everyday speech. Margaret Donaldson (1993) has characterized the kind of language found in text books as 'the language of systematised thought' and has pointed to the essential impersonal nature of this language, which comes detached from a personal reference and is not like the spoken word. As well as familiarity with story forms, pupils need to be read and also hear read many different kinds of information texts in order to understand how language operates in a variety of formal contexts.

Linguistic complexity of the information texts

In a study of a range of information texts used by the youngest readers, Frances Smith (1992), a LINC advisory teacher, points out that children 'have to learn a new kind of reading for information books, they need different kinds of reading for different factual genres'. Non-fiction books often contain complex sentences that are rarely found in children's speech and which make their appearance much later in children's own writing. These include the use of the passive voice and long series of prepositional phrases which tax a reader's short-term memory such as in the following example:

> In order to identify the furs of lawfully killed polar bears, Innuit or Eskimos, of the North West territories of Canada are issued with a quota of tags at the beginning of each winter's hunting season.

Some words are used in an unfamiliar sense, as in the way 'command' appears in the following statement:

> The polar bear's coat *commands* a significant price in the market place.

She also points out the text's frequent use of nominalization, whereby a verb meaning is transferred to a noun as in the example, 'In North America the *distribution* of brown bears overlaps with that of the American black bears'. This again is a technique that is not employed at all in story writing and which is rarely seen in children's own compositions until a later stage of development. In particular, books aimed at older primary children frequently assume a total familiarity with all the conventions of non-fiction and give no help to the less experienced reader. Smith concludes that teachers have a vital role to play in helping children gain control of this kind of reading skill through the careful selection of appropriate materials, adding that 'reading aloud and discussing books designed for older children can help to accustom them to language uses that may be unfamiliar'.

Teachers' strategies have often been to mediate the texts to their classes by summarizing for them information or selecting the particular details they wish them to use in project work. Some information texts for younger children deliberately adopt a simple narrative format or attempt to make the reading process easier by addressing the young reader in a register approximating to the patterns of children's speech in what Michael Marland has described in *The Guardian* as 'the curse of the vernacular' (*The Guardian*, 23 May 1991). Such short-term measures will not help children in the long term to deal with information texts independently.

In a more comprehensive survey of how children can be helped to find out about finding out, Bobby Neate has made a detailed analysis of differences in the kinds of narrative and expository texts used in schools and suggests that children rarely find exposition in their early readers. Information books are meant to be read in parts rather than continuous wholes and the illustrations also carry important information. The language of exposition often uses specific technical terms which may demand prior knowledge of the subject area from the reader. Neate also concludes that because both teachers and publishers have emphasized the importance of the visual impact of new information books, the attractiveness and utility of their illustrations and diagrams has been improved, without similar attention being given to either the quality of the writing or the lay-out of the print (Neate, 1992: 47–61).

The work of both Neate and Smith has important implications for the classroom. First, teachers need to be much more aware when selecting information texts for their projects of the kinds of textual organization that will facilitate their pupils' understanding and need to pressurize publishers for better books. Second, they need to understand that the books supplied in project collections present many difficulties for young readers who need to be provided with strategies for using them more effectively. This means that work needs to highlight the structures of particular information texts to prepare children for effective reading. The danger with the National Curriculum's new emphasis on good comprehension is that teachers may try to develop these complex research skills through structured exercises or library workshops divorced from real curriculum purposes for finding out and reporting back. When presented with the evidence from such surveys the teachers who had been involved in the development of work to promote narrative understanding at Key Stage 2 agree that, although they frequently used information books for project work, they often pre-selected particular sections of information prior to the work in class, or even solved the problems of difficult information texts by paraphrasing the information for their classes. This meant, in fact, they were short-cutting many of the steps required for personal research work and were giving children only a limited experience of using non-fiction to make new meanings for themselves.

Register

One of the key features that identifies the most effective readers is their ability to adapt rapidly to the register of a text and understand very quickly what sort of information they may expect from it. Adults, through their wide experience, have gradually accumulated a bank of registers and know, with varying skill, how to read or produce a range of writing. When faced with the need to use a new genre, for example when a graduate writes a first CV, or completes a letter of application for a professional job, the literate reader first looks to a competent model in order to shape their own response appropriately.

Similarly, in their reading, adults require only minimal cues to alert them to the kind of reading required to process the text because they are familiar with a wide range of genres and registers. Hasan (1980) who worked with M.A.K. Halliday on textual cohesion stresses the importance of a shared culture in shaping response to print and points out how text openings like, 'Once upon a time', 'In the beginning', 'Dear Sir' serve as important signals to the mature reader as to what kind of reading is required of them. In primary schools children read mainly fiction and are most frequently asked to write in a personal, chronological way, so that even when they are reporting project work they frequently do so from a personal point of view recounting what has occurred rather than offering description and analysis. This personal writing then spills over into other forms such as report writing even when the style is inappropriate. Examples can be found when children write up work undertaken in Science and Technology.

Paul (age 11) has constructed a waterwheel in Technology and describes his work, using diagrams appropriate to a scientific report. However he gives a personal recount of his experience, rather than a true report (Figure 7.1).

> First our group had to design a waterwheel. We decided that we would make a double waterwheel using plastic containers, drawing pins and balsa wood. We managed to work out how it could work. Then we had to mark the points for the pins. It took twenty drawing pins to make it but when we tried it out it did not work. We thought that the wheels that held it were too tight, so we tried to take them off but they were stuck. But when we took it to our teacher he said well done but don't carry on with it.

The passage opens in a business-like way and the main details of the waterwheel's construction are given but Paul's concern is to tell exactly what happened. He uses a simple chronological structure with active verbs in the simple past tense. The piece ends, like the project he is describing, with a feeling of incompleteness. In another piece, however, where Paul had researched an information book on the uses of wood, he manages an impersonal tone using the passive voice to produce a report more appropriate than his piece on the waterwheel (Figure 7.2).

> Wood is used for all sorts of things, such as furniture, firewood etc. Wood comes from trees, oak, pine and others. A long time ago a lot of ships would have been made out of wood. The 'Mary Rose' was made of oak and so was the 'HMS Victory'. The reason why they used wood for ships was because it floated. Fishing boats were made of oak too.

It might be argued that the latter represents a close copy of the original information, but there is enough evidence that Paul has re-organized some of the ideas in his own words. Material has been selected carefully and kept close to the language of the text so that Paul is learning to use a different genre effectively to convey general information with specific examples. There has been an overemphasis on making children write out the information they find

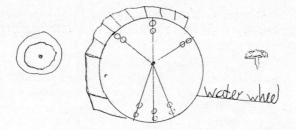

THE WATER WHEEL

First our group had to design a water wheel. We decided that we would make a double water wheel using plastic containers drawing pins and balsa wood. We managed to work out how it could work. Then we had to mark the points for the pins. It took 20 drawing pins to make it but when we tried it out it did not work. We thought that the wheels that held it were too tight, so we tried to take them off but they were stuck. But when we took it to our teacher he said well done but don,t carry on with it.

Figure 7.1 Paul's waterwheel

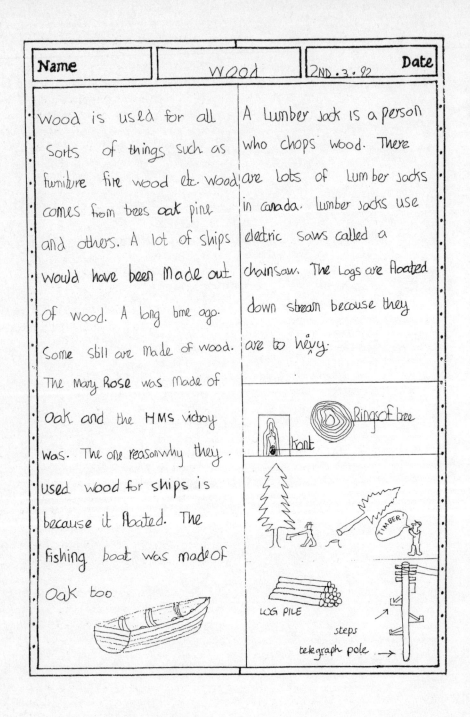

| Name | wood | 2ND . 3 . 92 | Date |

Wood is used for all sorts of things such as furniture fire wood etc. Wood comes from trees oak pine and others. A lot of ships would have been made out of wood. A long time ago. Some still are made of wood. The mary Rose was made of Oak and the HMS victory was. The one reason why they used wood for ships is because it floated. The fishing boat was made of Oak too

A Lumber Jack is a person who chops wood. There are lots of lumber Jacks in canada. lumber Jacks use electric saws called a chainsaw. The Logs are floated down stream because they are to heavy.

front

Rings of tree

TIMBER

LOG PILE

steps
telegraph pole →

Figure 7.2 Paul's project research on the uses of wood

in books in their own words (Littlefair, 1991: 98). What is more important than rewriting is that children get practice in using more formal registers in appropriate ways. Copying, when information has been selected appropriately, is the first stage to managing more complex linguistic structures. Most children lack this variety of reading experience in school contexts. On the whole, early methods of reading emphasize beginning at the first page and working your way through to the end. In order to be able to deal with other kinds of texts and to adapt to different registers children need to be shown how to use more information texts in the process of completing project work. Often the stress has been on the project content at the expense of methods of enquiry, and children are given insufficient practice in making proper use of non-narrative written forms. J.R. Martin's study (1989: 53–4) of Australian children's writing in primary school found that out of 1500 pieces that were collected, only 228 were factual writing. Moreover, good and average writers provided most of the reports, explanations and procedures; poor writers were doing almost no factual writing at all at this stage. Children in this country similarly encounter far fewer non-fiction texts in their school reading and recourse to personal information reading is rarely encouraged in classroom writing.

Sharing information texts in class

In making plans for implementing the reading requirements for the National Curriculum the teachers in the survey were determined to devise ways to help children become more aware of the organization and presentation of information in their reference books in a structured way. The children were quite accustomed to use books in topic work but were rarely asked directly to share their reading of non-fiction texts with either adults or other members of the class. The most usual way in which information was shared in class was for the teacher to explain what was being studied and to point out where particular children had produced interesting work. Children did not discuss their reading together although boys had described sharing information from the hobby magazines they brought from home.

The main problem, and one experienced in most schools working on projects, was that many children's only strategy when finding information was to copy large chunks of the texts they thought were relevant, without showing any personal understanding or selection of appropriate detail. In one of the group reading sessions, the children were therefore specifically asked to help identify which of the books provided in their latest project collection would be most useful for their current research into different kinds of plant life. Their first task was to brainstorm the kinds of information they might want to find out and list these in table form. They decided the following kinds of information would be most useful:

Flowering season
Whether garden or wild flower
Annual, perennial or biennial
Method of pollination
How cultivated
Native or foreign
Size of plant
Edible or poisonous
Conditions required for growth

They then worked in pairs skimming through particular books, not to answer their individual research questions such as 'Which plants are inedible?' but to assess if there were sufficient information in the text to deal with such enquiries. In order to complete the task they needed to look at contents pages, indexes, chapter headings and diagrams. Problems occurred when pairs could not find some of the information they needed but in discussion it was pointed out that some books were more informative on some of the aspects than others and they would need to select another book when they began their research in earnest.

They recorded their findings in matrix form (Figure 7.3). They then completed another matrix to record the specific details that they could find for individual plants (Figure 7.4). Their next task was to decide which aspect of the project was most interesting for them. The whole class helped to formulate the questions they wanted to answer such as

How are seeds spread and which seeds are spread in which way?
Where do different flowers live?
How does a bulb grow?
How do animals pollinate plants?

Their next task was to consider the most useful book for the question they were currently considering and to work on a particular topic which they would be asked to share with others in the group later. While recounting the information they had researched to each other they would not be allowed to refer back to the book or read out the passages from the text, but would be expected to summarize the information verbally. This would show how well they had understood what they had been reading. In order to help them remember what they had read they were asked to pick out the main points and jot down keywords. The latter proved a very difficult task for them. Many of them started to copy out whole chunks of the texts without selecting key points as they had been accustomed to do in previous projects. The teacher decided to give more help in identifying the key ideas. She photocopied specific parts of the textbooks related to specific questions and then showed the class how to underline connecting details in the passages to identify the main ideas. These

Title of Book	Wild Flowers Bob Gibbons	Flowers Burnie. D.	Garden Flowers Swallow' SU	Wild Flowers Jim Flegg	Indoor plants Leslie Johns
Flower	✓	✓	✓	✓	✓
Poisonous	✓		✓	✓	
Size	✓		✓	✓	
Flowering Season		✓		✓	
Edible	✓	✓		✓	✓
Rare	✓	✓		✓	
Native, foreign	✓	✓	✓	✓	✓
Hardy	✓	✓	✓	✓	
Planting Season		✓	✓		✓
Indoors/ outdoors	✓	✓	✓	✓	✓
Bulb, seed cutting		✓	✓		✓
Wild/ cultivated	✓	✓	✓	✓	✓
Pollination	✓	✓			
Annual, Perennial		✓			
Berries	✓	✓	✓	✓	

Figure 7.3 A matrix to show which books would be useful for particular enquiries

Daffodil	Sun Flower	Dandelion	Name of Plant
Yes	Yes	Yes	Flower
Yes	NO	NO	Poisonous
15-60cm	1.5-2.8 meters	5-30cm	Size
spring	Sumer	october march	Flowering Season
NO	yes	NO	Edible
NO	NO	NO	Rare
both	native	Native	Native/foreign
NO	NO	NO	Hardy
o	spring summer		Planting Season
outdoors	outdoors	outdoors	Indoors/Outdoors
bulb	Seed	Seed	Bulb, seed, cutting
cultivated	cultivated	wild	Wild/cultivated
yes	NO	yes	Pollination
Annual Perennial	Annual	Annual	Annual, Perennial
no	no	no	Berries

Figure 7.4 Matrix 2. Information given about particular plants

were then recorded in a picture format so that they could be used as an *aide-mémoire* for the presentation. The emphasis was on understanding information and reporting it in a new way rather than copying ideas down in the same format.

Louise and Charlotte's work on how seeds are spread is represented in Figure 7.5.

Lauren and Crystal also produced records of their research (Figure 7.6). In structuring the learning process in this way, the teacher was directing the children's attention to specific aspects of the text in the way Directed Activities Related to Texts (DART) were recommended by the Schools Council project on learning in the Humanities (Davies, 1986). DART's activities help children to categorize, evaluate and process texts, in order to make their own use of the information they find. The analytical work then leads to group discussion so that further research can be carried out.

The children's familiarity with the narrative structures of their story books helped them to realize some of the books they used for information were also organized like stories. In the class library collection they found stories of Napoleon's campaigns, stories of Florence Nightingale and stories about Antarctic expeditions. They decided that many true stories were written about people and their achievements and that fiction and information books could sometimes have similar structures, just as in previous work on ways of telling stories they had found some poems which told stories, such as *The Highwayman* and *The Lady of Shallot*. In this way they were beginning to develop a schemata of the range of different kinds of writing they encountered in and outside school and the different ways of reading or using the texts.

The children's interrogation of their information books was based on the same principle as the way in which they had learned to ask questions as a class about their fiction books. The teacher began from the prior knowledge that children had built up about non-fiction lower down the school and worked to expand these concepts through sharing information and formalizing their understanding in class sessions. In a brainstorm conducted after the first survey of the project collection, they were able to identify the features of information books which helped them use the books effectively. They decided on the following features:

Information books

Have an index arranged in alphabetical order
Have a list of contents arranged in page order
Have sections, chapters, headings, sub-headings
Have realistic illustrations or photographs which are important for giving information
Sometimes have glossaries which explained new terms used in the text
Sometimes have more than one author and an editor or compiler
Are not necessarily read from front to back
Are not often in a story form

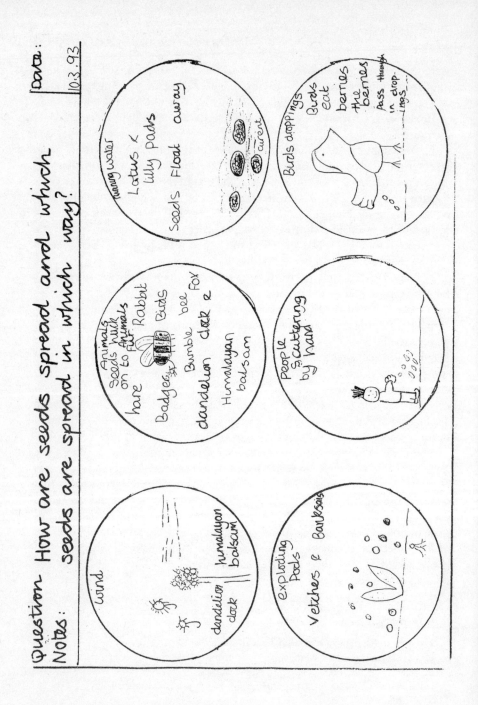

Figure 7.5 First Louise and Charlotte identified which plants were spread in particular ways and then constructed their diagram to show the main details

Question were do different plants grow?
Notes:

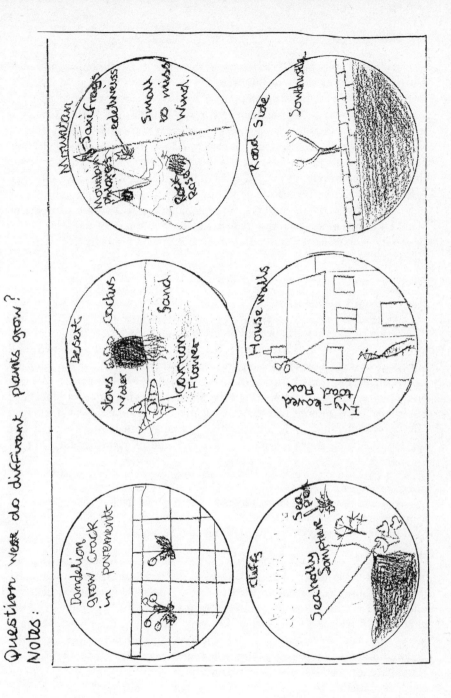

Figure 7.6 Lauren and Crystal researched the different habitats of plants

The children were helped to identify all these features in the books they were using and to employ some of their features in their own subsequent research writing. In their next topic on shipping they used the matrix format again to identify the areas that they wanted to follow up in their own writing, choosing more narrative areas such as 'famous sailors, great voyages and shipwrecks'.

The class teacher considered that the initial survey of the book collection helped them to choose the topics which they were able to research and gave the class teacher an insight into which areas of the topic needed better resourcing.

One unexpected outcome of the survey of the books about plants was that they identified one of the authors as someone whose books were particularly helpful. D. Burnie was an author they particularly approved of and some of the class went independently and found other information books by this writer in the school library.

Working with newspapers

The different linguistic features of other common genres were also examined in detail. For example, the teachers recognized that many children when they are asked to write a newspaper report used familiar personal narrative forms, re-organizing the presentation format into the shape of newspaper columns, but applying none of the other linguistic features or conventions of reporting. In his 'newspaper account' of a school residential visit to Slimbridge, Christopher (11) has invented a suitably journalistic headline 'Youth Hostel Disaster' but the accompanying copy is really a personal recount of events (Figure 7.7).

> Would you like to be a teacher? Here are some things you have to cope with. For example, vomit. Peter went to bed at 11.00 p.m. on Monday. Everybody was talking and he had a bad headache. Paul and Craig were fighting and this made it worse. Peter went into the wash room and started crying. He stopped crying at last and went back to bed but at 4 a.m. he woke up and was sick.'

The 'article' develops over a further three columns with much detail about who said what to whom and finishing with a nose bleed on the bus the next day. The register is more appropriate to that of a personal journal and lacks the kind of factual detail appropriate to newspapers. In fact a large number of the children did not read a newspaper at home and were unfamiliar with their layout. In order to develop a better understanding of newspaper style, the children examined how a variety of newspapers were organized and discussed the differences between the items found on the front and inside pages in an early introduction to the concept of news values. They were shown how to locate facts in the text quickly by skimming and scanning. When they had spent time looking at a full range of tabloid and broadsheet publications they were given the first paragraph of the newspaper and asked to see if they could find:

SLIMBRIDGE STORIES

YOUTH HOSTEL DISASTERS

Would you like to be a teacher? Here are some things you have to cope with. For example, Vomit. Peter _____ went to bed at 11.00pm on Monday. Everyone was talking and he had a bad headache. Paul _____ and Craig _____ were fighting, and that was making it worse. Peter went into the wash room and started to cry. He stopped crying and went back to bed. Peter got to sleep at last but he woke up at 4.00am and he was sick. Peter said to Paul _____ and Adam _____ "Go and get Mr H _____". When Mr H _____ came he was half asleep, and did not know where to find anything to clean it up with, so he just put paper towels over it until the morning. When Peter woke up in the morning, Mr N _____ got an empty chocolate box and scraped up most of the sick, and then he put sawdust over it and hoovered it up. The next day we went for a long walk, we walked about 4 miles. We got back at the hostel at 10.30pm. Martin _____ was just laying in bed awake, when there was a shower of blood out of his nose. Paul told Mr H _____ Mr

H _____ came in and said "What's the matter" Martin said "My nose is bleeding" Mr H _____ helped Martin down from his bed. He asked David _____ to get some tissues out of his bag. Martin put the tissues over his nose and pinched it. After that he walked into the washroom and bathed his nose with cold water. The next day Alex _____ woke up at 4.00am. His face felt wet and slippery, so he looked at his pillow and there was a pool of blood from his nose. He got out of bed and went to the washroom and bathed it with cold water, and when it had stopped bleeding he went back to bed. The next day he had to change all his sheets, which were now red instead of green. He went for a walk after breakfast and he was walking with Mrs H _____ and his friends, when it started bleeding again. Then Brian the bus driver gave Alex some tissues to wipe the blood off, but it had stopped bleeding. The day after, Alex had yet another nose bleed while everybody was looking at Shakespeares birth place.

By Christopher _____ and David _____

THE MOORHEN'S NEST

While we were looking at the flamingos, Mr H _____ spotted one of the hundreds of moorhens, squatting down in a clump of grass. As he and Peter _____ approached it, the bird walked off, revealing a nest of twigs with two large eggs in it. When we approached the nest the next day the mother got up and walked away for the second day running but suprisingly this time there were three eggs. The eggs were a dirty white with brown speckles. As soon we had left the nest the mother ran back to her nest and started to incubate the nest again.

Paul _____ and Michael _____

BRIAN SAVES BUS ON MOTORWAY

On the way back from the trip to Slimbridge, Brian the bus driver used his quick reactions to save some of the pupis from Hempshill Hall School. There was a pile up of cars, eight to be exact. Brian saw these cars and he swerved around them everyone on the bus fell out of their seats. Bobby _____, a pupil from Hempshill Hall was asleep, and the swerve threw him out of his seat and on to the floor. He banged his head and the force woke him up.

Paul _____ and Michael _____

Figure 7.7 'Youth hostel disasters'

What had happened?
Who was involved?
Where had the incident happened?
When had it happened? and (if any reason had been given)
Why it had happened?

They were asked to underline the details and then compare them with other reports of the same incident in another paper. These were referred to as the 'five Ws' of reporting and the children were encouraged to include these in the newspaper articles they produced for a classroom newspaper. A visitor to the school, observing their work, contributed the following quotation from Kipling as an *aide-mémoire*:

I keep six honest servingmen
(they taught me all I knew)
Their names are
What and Why and When and
How and Where and Who

In the following opening, taken from his contribution to the class paper, Christopher begins with an appropriate journalistic style, although, unpractised in a difficult genre, he quickly slips into a personal recount.

On the 10th of June 20 pupils from H.H. Primary School went to London Miss Morris and Miss Brown went with them. We left school at 7.35 a.m. on the coach . . .

The teacher decided the problem mainly arose because the reporters had been part of the outing and so could not distance themselves sufficiently from the events they were describing, hence the first-person pronouns and the subjective viewpoint. She therefore gave the children some practice in 'reporting' the views of others in the form of newspaper language so that they could become familiar with the passive voice and reported speech. They highlighted sentences in the papers that used these constructions and then practised using them in their own writing. They also made a study of headlines and noticed the kind of language used to grab their attention, inventing their own headlines, which used the conventions of punning and condensation, typical of the press, such as the following account of a cricketing incident, 'A Stinging Report' in which David reports an encounter with nettles using appropriate subheadings, 'Child Falls in Nettles' and 'On Your Knees' (Figure 7.8).

This example shows how children have difficulty at this stage with passive forms. The young journalists all prefer to use direct speech rather than the passive voice of reported comment.

HEMPSHILL MAIL JUNE EDITION

A STINGING SPORT

CHILD FALLS IN NETTLES

The children poured out of Stratford youth hostel on to the garden to play cricket. David was in field first. Then when David was waiting to bat Mrs. B____ took a group to play ball games. Then David tried to do an over head scisser kick and landed in some nettles and he was almost crying then he took a quick bath and in the morning he was o.k.

DAVID

David said, "It was painful all over" and he was almost crying after having stinging marks on his back, legs and arms.

ON YOUR KNEES

Robert ____ was in bat. Paul J. hit the ball and Robert was running until he sprained his knee. Robert said "It felt painful!" but he walked back to the hostel.

BALL UP A TREE

Mr. H____ took a group of children to play football. As he was playing, Andrew ____ kicked the ball up a tree then David ____ got a leg up the tree to shake the bratch to get the ball down then we carried on playing the game.

By Robert ____ and Louis ____

 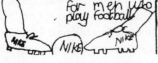 

Figure 7.8 'A stinging sport'

The language of marketing

In another Y6 class, the children undertook a survey of marketing techniques concentrating on consumer packaging as their starting point for their investigation of the devices manufacturers and advertisers use to persuade customers to pick their product from the shelf. In their analyses they looked at the choice of words in the naming of products, as well as the general design of the packaging and the way information was set out and combined with images to create a particular effect. Their understanding of the information carried by packaging and the devices used to catch a consumer's attention, was shown in poster analyses. They had discussed how the style of print might reflect the meaning of brand names as well as the connotations suggested in both the language and images selected for particular products. They then used the knowledge they had gained from their analyses to create their own products, design packages and advertise them using a video and VCR to make television commercials. In scripting these and making sure they were read out accurately and with appropriate expression they were also gaining further practice in reading aloud using a genre other than narrative, to put over ideas.

These ways of working seemed to the teachers involved to be allowing them to help children towards making explicit their understanding of different forms of textual organization. Each activity drew upon children's prior learning and encouraged them to articulate what they already knew before adding to their understanding.

When a lack of knowledge of a particular genre or textual form was discovered the teachers provided further examples of that particular genre so that the children gained more knowledge of that particular way of organizing writing.

The areas that were covered in these activities included:

- Brainstorming from prior knowledge to create a context for learning.
- Formulating their own questions to direct their research.
- Finding the main idea in a passage by underlining.
- Looking for linking ideas (lexical chains).
- Using matrices to collate information.
- Mapping, a method similar to brainstorming but using ideas found within a text rather than prior knowledge.
- Modelling, i.e. representing ideas that have been researched in a graphic form.

The main emphasis was on allowing the children to find their own way into reading tasks with careful support from the teacher who shaped their learning by finding real purposes for reading and suggesting appropriate genres and audiences for communicating the information gathered. Of the children interviewed in the following year at their secondary schools it was these who most often expressed a disappointment that they no longer were involved in researching topic work in their lessons. Significantly too, they were the ones who reported using the school library to find information for their own interests, as did Helen, for instance, who used the library to find information to help her sort out her problems with a sick hamster.

Record keeping and assessment

The children kept copies of their research notes, drafts and matrices in their reading portfolios so that the teacher could use their work for a basis for discussion when conducting reading conferences and include their work with information in the records of reading achievement (see Chapter 8). The combination of writing based on the reading, records of contributions to reading conferences, detailed individual records of the books read and the comment books created a bank of evidence for the children's final reading assessment which I will discuss in greater detail in the following chapter.

Reading across the Curriculum Key Stage 3

The interviews I conducted with the children in their first year of secondary school were therefore particularly disappointing because most of the reading tasks described had narrative or poetry as the main focus and were part of work in English lessons. Very few children could name books that they had been asked to read as part of other areas of the curriculum and most suggested the reading was mainly provided by worksheets prepared by their teachers that required recall of information explained in the class or answering questions from a single textbook in subjects such as Geography and History.

Christine's experience of reading in secondary school subject specialisms, described in Chapter 5, represents the norm for her age group.

This adds weight to the importance of giving sufficient attention during Key Stage 2 to more advanced reading skills to prepare sufficiently for independent study. It also suggests that subject teachers at Key Stage 3 need to reconsider how the development of subject-related reading skills can be integrated into their classroom practice. Many of the librarians in the secondary schools I visit suggest that many children only learn to use the library effectively when they are faced with coursework in GCSE in Y10 and 11. The English teachers whom I interviewed were aware of the limited reading their pupils were being asked to do in other areas of the curriculum and had begun to introduce ways of recording other forms of reading that pupils experienced outside the English lessons. Their findings reinforced my impressions that many children's experience of non-fiction is very limited:

'As a department we've been working on a reading record to try and identify what the children are reading outside school on what we call a regular basis – that means perhaps most weeks – and there we're encouraging them to write about magazines, comics, *Radio Times*, the *TV Times*, anything that they read regularly and to try and identify with a particular magazine what aspects of that

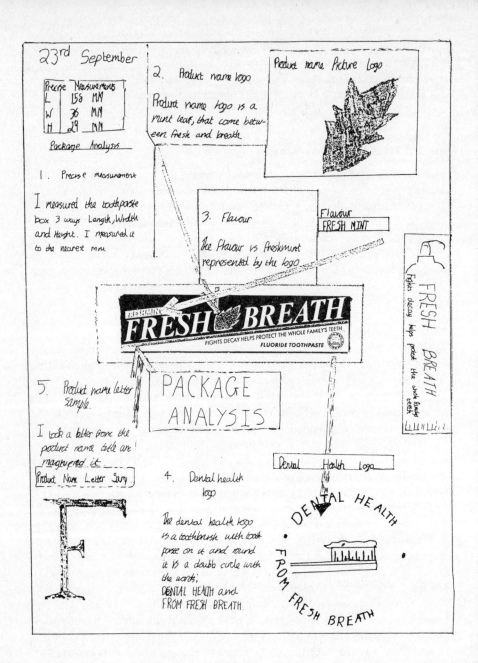

Figure 7.9 Package analysis

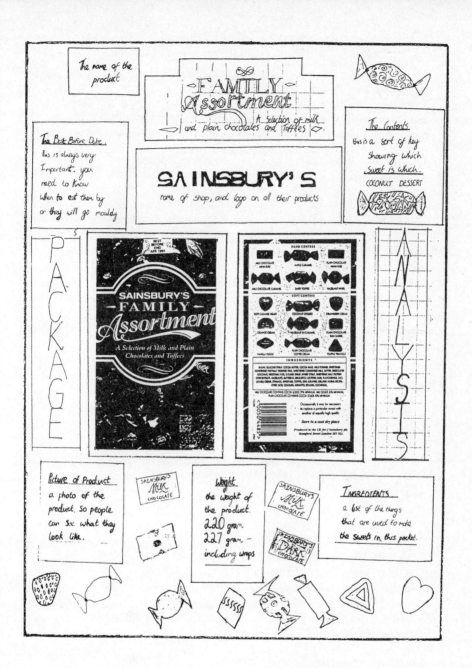

The name of the product

FAMILY Assortment
A selection of milk and plain chocolates and Toffees.

SAINSBURY'S
name of shop, and logo on all their products

The Best Before Date. This is always very Important. you need to Know when to eat them by or they will go mouldy

The Contents this is a sort of key Showing which sweet is which. COCONUT DESSERT

PACKAGE

ANALYSIS

Picture of Product a photo of the product, so people can See what they look like.

Weight the weight of the product. 220 gram 227 gram - including wraps

SAINSBURY'S Milk CHOCOLATE

SAINSBURY'S Milk CHOCOLATE

SAINSBURY'S DARK CHOCOLATE

INGREDIENTS a list of the things that are used to make the sweets in this packet.

Figure 7.9

magazine they enjoy and read most, for example, do they read about fashion, do they look at reviews, is it hobbies or the stars? Whatever it may be, that will then give us some feedback on the kind of non-fictional reading they're doing outside school. At the same time the reading record will include all the books that they are reading within English lessons. What's beginning to emerge at this early stage is that most of the reading that they record on their reading record is fictional. Although there is a column for non-fiction reading, it's very rarely at the moment ticked.

English teachers at Key Stage 3 are beginning to collate information about the broad sweep of children's reading interests and experiences, but this is probably insufficient to ensure that children are using reading as a tool for learning throughout the curriculum. It is much easier in the later stages of the primary school to lay the foundations for the effective use of reading skills, as well as ensuring that all children are introduced to the pleasure of imaginative writing in poetry and prose. The children in this study kept records of all the books they read in class and the selections from their writing in other formats also enabled their teachers to assess what kinds of texts they had been able to use effectively.

Conclusions

1 It is important to analyse the kinds of books provided for children's re-search work in project collections and ensure that they provide adequate guidance for learning. Teachers should allow children to work with the information texts, rather than selecting material for them in the process Margaret Meek (Meek, 1992) calls 'work-sheet matching.'
Children need help to develop flexible reading habits when finding out information. These include the ability to:
   • skim for general impressions
   • scan for detail
   • identify key points in texts
   • record information in a variety of ways
2 Activities are required that help children to understand the way informa-tion texts are constructed and to help them to get information from:
   • blurbs
   • tables of content
   • indexes
   • illustrations and diagrams
   • headings and sub-headings
   • glossaries
3 Children need help in learning how to devise questions which will direct their own reading activity. Teachers working on projects need to teach the process of finding out as well as emphasizing the importance of the content of the written work.

4 Note-taking is a complex skill which Key Stage 2 children find difficult, but which they can be helped to develop by being asked to underline or highlight particular details and then re-organize the information that they have identified as most important.

5 Teachers need to be aware of the demands made on readers by information texts and develop work which helps pupils familiarize themselves with more complex forms of textual organization.

6 Teachers should provide opportunities for children to work in a variety of registers and ensure that the information books they select do not mainly convey information in a narrative form.

7 Reading records should contain details about the kind of non-fiction each child has used and those genres which they choose to read voluntarily.

8 Children's reading material provides models for their own writing so that information books should also be chosen and recommended with a view to their role in extending pupils' writing repertoire. Girls in particular need more encouragement to choose non-fictional texts as part of their personal reading.

9 Children need to be given a range of writing tasks which create the possibility of using a variety of registers. It is important to point out the appropriate features of descriptive, rather than narrative, reports.

10 In the secondary school, specialist teachers need to plan for reading within their specialism and be prepared to point out the significant discourse features and technical vocabulary associated with their subject. In the middle years children's reading records need to make more provision for reading in areas of the curriculum other than English.

8 How should children's reading be assessed?

Everyday literacy always has a purpose. We should therefore be aware that tests which isolate literacy from context, and even those which merely simulate a context are probably misrepresenting learners' abilities or needs.

R. Ivanic and H. Hamilton, 1990

Before we, as teachers rather than examiners, set about deciding how to assess children's reading, it is important to clarify the reasons why we are being asked to make assessments and then ask ourselves what use will be made of the information we record. For the past five years assessment issues have dominated schools' agendas in the UK because one major aim of the National Curriculum, set up by the Education Reform Act 1988, was to place assessment at the centre of the curriculum. To support assessment, the Task Group on Assessment and Testing (TGAT) was appointed in July 1987 to advise Secretaries of State and its main report published in the following December recommended the 10-level scale for pupil assessment which was rapidly accepted and now dominates the structure of all National Curriculum subject planning. It also advocated two ways of assessing achievement, first through continuous teacher assessment throughout the key stage and second through nationally set tasks or tests, carried out at the end of the key stage.

The TGAT report described teacher assessment as being part of everyday teaching and learning, not as a separate activity which would require extra tasks or tests. Such assessments were intended to be developed from the kind of professional judgements about children's attainments that teachers made in the course of planning and developing work. It was stressed that the recording of attainment throughout each key stage was intended to be helpful in planning for the next stage of learning and it was also recommended that children should be involved in charting their own progress.

These principles, based on a teaching cycle which uses assessment to diagnose what needs to be taught next, reflect the current best practice of most teachers. However, the continuous formative aspects of the assessment process have been rapidly overshadowed by the Standard Assessments prescribed for the end of each stage of learning. In the beginning, these too were intended to mirror the kinds of tasks teachers might set in a particular learning context. However, they have quickly developed into more formal tests. Their focus now appears to have more to do with establishing the relative performance of schools in league tables and to providing methods of comparing national standards from year to year. The latter intention was particularly evident in the way that the first reported results of the Standard Assessment Tasks (SATs) for seven-year olds were used by both the national press and politicians to criticize standards of early reading and by extension, the methods of teaching reading, particularly what was perceived as a neglect of phonic instruction. No evidence however was found for the claims of the tabloid press, that teachers of infants do not know how to teach reading effectively or that reading instruction has become dominated by a 'real book method' at the expense of phonic instruction. On the contrary, both local and national school inspections, have shown that in the early years, not only do all teachers place a high priority on the teaching of reading, but most also use a mixture of methods which includes work on phonics as well as an introduction to stories.

Where a decline in reading attainment has been found, the evidence points to socio-economic factors depressing children's performance, rather than any difference in the kind of reading instruction provided. For example in 'Reading in Recession', a report that received very little press coverage, the NFER found that though there had been a significant fall in average standard scores in reading between 1987 and 1991 and lower standards were not general throughout the system. In fact, some schools registered an improvement in reading but all these schools were in county, rural or middle-class suburbs of cities. The research team found no significant association between the methods of instruction and the pupils' attainment. The lowering of results may therefore be associated with increases in the extent of childhood poverty, since there is strong research evidence that links the quality of a child's home life and reading ability.

What can be confirmed, however, is that teachers themselves have placed less emphasis on the monitoring and assessment of individual children's reading than other aspects of the curriculum and few schools can provide a detailed overview of their pupil's performance. The Nottinghamshire survey (Nottinghamshire Advisory and Inspection Service and Educational Psychology Service, 1991) found 'Very few schools reported using any systematic approaches to monitoring the effectiveness of teaching reading and most schools were unable to provide evidence of trends in reading achievement'. Schools relied mainly on the judgement and experience of the teachers in their observations of children's reading behaviour.

Teachers have therefore had difficulty in providing concrete evidence of the kind of development they are fostering in day-to-day teaching and it is this aspect of assessment that has a key role to play, not only in helping children understand their own learning, but in informing parents of progress and en-gaging their co-operation.

My own survey also found that many children judge their achievement in reading in comparison with others largely by calculating the number of books they read in a term, the size of the print in the books they choose and their ability to concentrate for longer stretches in periods set aside for silent reading. Most children were encouraged to record the number of pages they read in a session, sometimes supplementing this with some comment on their response to the book in terms of simple preference. Parents' comments on their children's reading were also often invited and used by teachers to broaden their picture of children's motivation and attitudes to reading at home.

Such records of what children are reading are important indicators of the range and breadth of their reading interests but on their own they provide a very limited picture of an individual's reading development and offer little opportunity for comparison between classes. This is because teacher assess-ments, based on implicit understanding of what it is to be a 'good reader', lack a shared framework within which individual assessments can be understood and compared. What teacher assessment comes down to in many cases is a reliance on judgements based on the complexity of the kinds of texts that the pupil has chosen to read. There is, however, in all aspects of teaching, a need for some way of recording successful learning through a common set of standards. Teachers need to keep more detailed evidence of their pupils' at-tainment if they wish to argue for continuous teacher assessment rather than simplistic tests of limited skills. Adequate records which facilitate transition between the different phases of education are best achieved by teacher as-sessments based on agreed criteria and shared processes of recording.

A pupil's reading can never be successfully assessed by a one-off test, however attractive the notion of pencil-and-paper assessment appears to be to politicians. Written responses to questions on de-contextualized reading ma-terial are the least attractive or reliable way of finding out about global reading ability. The assessment of reading needs to be part of the teaching cycle and its purpose should be to help both teacher and pupil form an all-round picture of the learner's growing ability to make sense of a wide range of reading tasks, while identifying areas for further growth. The emphasis therefore needs to be switched from setting tests on a particular occasion once a year, to identifying the kinds of information that teachers and pupils can collect over time in order to create a comprehensive picture of individual achievement.

Creating a portfolio of reading

Portfolios of children's writing which are evidence of their growing control of the written language are now commonplace and it is equally practicable to gather a portfolio of evidence about each individual's reading. This portfolio might include:

- teacher's log of observations in different context, e.g. when children read their own work to others;
- systematic records of pupil–teacher reading conferences;
- samples of passages selected for reading aloud to other children, parents or teachers, with comments;
- a comment book or journals shared by teacher, parent and reader;
- children's own records of the books they have read;
- children's reviews of particular genres of writing, e.g. poetry and non-fiction as well as stories.

It is important to stress that it is not necessary to collect evidence of achievement in everything a pupil does or to keep the same piece of evidence for each child, but that the examples selected should provide support for particular judgements in a variety of learning contexts.

Sampling reading in other languages

Bilingual children may be reading extensively in their home language. It is important that this information is also recorded and children's reading of other literatures given credit when assessing the range and breadth of individual reading experience. Being able to read fluently in one language supports learning to read in another. Bilingual children may have a more sophisticated awareness of narrative style and story structure than their competence in English as their second language allows them to show. A community language teacher who can work in both languages can help bring this experience into the classroom. Older pupils who share a community language with a younger reader can also be helpful in accessing this sort of knowledge.

Teacher and pupil assessments

Recording personal preferences and range of reading experience

Teacher and pupil assessment should be thought of as a continuous process forming part of everyday teaching and learning. It should not involve specially devised activities. In Chapter 5 I have described a range of opportunities created by a Y6 teacher for her class to keep continuous records of their reading preferences in more detail and you will find examples of the methods of recording included there. They involved structured questionnaires, some of which were used as the basis of a reading conference with each pupil from which she was able to assess individual reading progress, make recommendations for wider reading and suggest targets for future development. Such records allow the teacher not only to make informed judgements about each reader's attitudes and motivation to the task but also to share her observations with others. These records were also used to show how well children understood the structure and functions of different elements of the book such as the blurb on the cover, its index and contents page. In addition, photocopied formats were used to share children's classroom reading experience directly with parents as part of the comment book and this helped the teacher to build records of the kind of reading experienced at home as well as in school.

Louise recorded this in her comment book (the words in italics were photocopied and stuck in each child's comment book by the teacher):

> *Today we practised a passage from one of our books that had speech in and then we read it aloud to a friend and then to a group.* I was good at: making expression and the rest of the group said I read quite loudly and fluently.
> *I need to improve at*: not speaking into the book and looking at the audience more often and stopping at full stops as well as reading a bit slower.

Later Louise's mother wrote:

> Louise read the first chapter of *Tales of a Fourth Grade Nothing* out loud to me. No problems – she's read it before apparently. She says there aren't any books left at school that she wants to read. Is she allowed to bring books from home? She would like to read *The Hobbit*.

The teacher replied:

> *The Hobbit* is a great idea. Louise managed to find another Judy Blume book that she liked and is happy again! I said that next time she chooses a book I will help her.

Lauren wrote this when asked to comment on her choice of poetry:

> I have read *Heard it in the Playground* by Alan Ahlberg. It doesn't have verses and it, only rhymes sometimes. It didn't change at the end but it repeated lines. My poem didn't have full stops. It was very long and Emma got bored. It made us laugh because it had made up words like 'Bum-shuka um' and 'jug ear, carrot top and pea brain'.

Lauren's mum added:

> Lauren's read me a few poems and has also finished *Charlie and the Chocolate Factory*.

The teacher responded:

> I've asked Lauren about her choice of books especially *Halloween*, as she has had it for a long time – she still seems keen to keep it. She likes the poetry book because it rhymes and she likes long poems too.

Wesley's mother who had some anxieties about his reading ability wrote:

> Wesley does like to read his *Look In* [a magazine] every week. He takes about three days before he finally puts it down. He goes through it very thoroughly.

He still tends to be lazy when it comes to reading his books but at the moment he is reading *The Story of Tracey Beaker*. He seems to be enjoying it. I have asked him about his reading wallet. It is bulging with books and so I have told him to take some out and just concentrate on a couple at a time. His report was pleasing. I agree what you say about his spelling. When he was doing his impact [Maths] about the garden he asked if 'path' was spelt 'p-a-f'! I do worry about it.

The teacher replied:

If you want some spelling ideas for him to do at home with you, pop in. Thanks for the very helpful comments.

Wesley wrote:

Today I read *Bill's New Frock*. I was attracted by the cover and the size of the print and the book is true to life. The main events are about a boy who woke up one day to find that he had to put on a frock. I like this book because it has things in that we do at school.

The teacher added:

Wesley is talking to me regularly about his reading – he is really keen at the moment – great – I've got the spelling work ready for you.

The three-way dialogue encouraged by the joint responsibility for, and exchange of, the comment book, allows the teacher to piece together a more comprehensive picture of the child's interests and reading habits and to recruit the parent's support for development in specific areas of learning. Where parents are unable or unwilling to give this kind of support from home, extra time can be provided in school to record the interests and responses of individuals.

These elements were supplemented in the children's reading folder with one or two photocopied examples of passages that children had selected to read aloud with their comments on how they had used their voice to create meaning and the strategies they had employed to engage the listener's attention taken from the comment books. In Chapter 4, I also suggested that children's writing, whether in direct response to a written text or as a piece of creative writing might also be used as evidence of reading experience and their understanding of story structure. Narratives are particularly useful if the teacher adds a note at the time about the nature of the writing task set. Similarly, the notes made by children in response to research tasks can serve as evidence of their ability to select main points from a non-fiction text, whether these are recorded in a visual or a written format.

Assessing children's reading strategies

Teachers also need to target some of the times they spend hearing children read to record the strategies they have developed for dealing with unfamiliar material and unknown vocabulary. This is particularly important for those children who are making slower progress than their peer group and who need greater help in developing their reading strategies. It can, however, also help the more accomplished reader gain an insight into strategies for reading more effectively

The *Primary Language Record* (Barrs *et al.*, 1988) which was produced by teachers in collaboration with the staff at the Centre for Language in Primary Education, provides a comprehensive framework for reading conferences with children and their parents. It is based on well-structured interviews with both the child and the parent and has an underlying framework of reading development which guides teachers in making their judgements. Two scales were developed to help the teacher plot children's progress. The first developed for top infants (Y2) uses a five-point scale to assess the beginner's development from dependence to independence as a reader. The second scale, reproduced below, charts the older pupil's development from inexperienced to experienced reader and was designed particularly to record the widening experience of the 9–11-year age range. They are recommended for use with whole classes of children annually or at particular transition points in their education to obtain an overall picture of a particular group and to evaluate reading policy in the light of this information (Barrs and Thomas, 1991: 108).

The *Primary Language Record* also suggests using running records or miscue analyses for identifying the pattern of a child's errors in a more formal way in order to identify the best strategy for further support.

Even when such time-consuming procedures are not part of the teacher's intentions for a particular reading session with a child, it is useful to look for, and note down, evidence that children have developed effective ways of dealing with new words or textual structures. Rather than listening to children read in an unfocused way, the teacher organizes paying attention to specific aspects of the individual's learning and records the details of the reading session. A shared comment book is a very convenient way of recording such a dialogue.

A reading conference

This should provide:

- Sufficient time for extended discussion of the books chosen by the child.
- A check that the child's selection includes at least one choice that can be read independently and none is at the level of reading frustration.
- The use of appropriate questions to help the child make predictions and hypotheses about the content of what is being read.
- Ways for the teacher and child to negotiate the next stages in the individual's reading programme and agree new targets.
- Instruction in appropriate reading strategies which include:

Experience as a reader across the curriculum: Reading Scale 2

1 Inexperienced reader	Experience as a reader has been limited. Generally chooses to read very easy and familiar texts where illustrations play an important part. Has difficulty with any unfamiliar material and yet may be able to read own dictated texts confidently. Needs a great deal of support with the reading demands of the classroom. Over-dependent on one strategy when reading aloud; often reads word by word. Rarely chooses to read for pleasure.
2 Less experienced reader	Developing fluency as a reader and reading certain kinds of material with confidence. Usually chooses short books with simple narrative shapes and with illustrations and may read these silently; often re-reads favourite books. Reading for pleasure often includes comics and magazines. Needs help with the reading demands of the classroom and especially with using reference and information books.
3 Moderately experienced reader	A confident reader who feels at home with books generally, reads silently and is developing stamina as a reader. Is able to read for longer periods and cope with more demanding texts, including children's novels. Willing to reflect on reading and often uses reading in own learning. Selects books independently and can use information books and materials for straightforward reference purposes, but still needs help with unfamiliar material, particularly non-narrative prose.
4 Experienced reader	A self-motivated, confident and experienced reader who may be pursuing particular interests through reading. Capable of tackling some demanding texts and can cope well with the reading demands of the curriculum. Reads thoroughly and appreciates shades of meaning. Capable of locating and drawing on a variety of sources in order to research a topic independently.
5 Exceptionally experienced reader	An enthusiastic and reflective reader who has strong established tastes in fiction and/or non-fiction. Enjoys pursuing own reading interests independently. Can handle a wide range and variety of texts, including adult material. Recognizes that different types of text require different styles of reading. Able to evaluate evidence drawn from a variety of information sources. Is developing critical awareness as a reader.

Source: *The Primary Language Record* (Barrs et al., 1988).

reading on to see what comes next;
reading back to see if that helps with the meaning;
making a best guess using the initial sound and context cues;
dividing a long word into significant parts and tackling it bit by bit.

Collecting reading histories

Teachers meeting children at the beginning of their secondary schooling may wish to supplement the transfer records of each child's reading provided by the primary school with their own reading conference. This helps the new teacher to form a more comprehensive picture of the pupil's attitudes and experience. The reading story format devised by one school working with the project helped individual pupils to recall the key stages of their own reading by writing histories of the ways they remembered learning to read and by recording their attitudes and preferences.

Keith's story (Figure 8.1) not only indicates the kinds of books that he wants to read but also gives his teacher some insight into books enjoyed in the primary school, *Carrie's War*, *Tyke Tiler*, *Danny: Champion of the World*, which might form the basis for further dialogue or help the teacher make new recommendations. The teacher might also want to follow up the disparity between Keith's report of wide reading experience with his lack of accuracy in spelling some common words like 'thik', 'pictor', 'exsiting', 'redding'.

Tests of reading comprehension

It is still a common practice in the middle years of school to train children to work through a series of short passages with questions to develop reading comprehension. The class routine is for each child to rule a margin, put the date and with head down work in isolation and blissful (for the teacher) silence for a whole period answering questions on a short passage. The work is decontextualized and seen as a form of practice rather than a purposeful task. Children become skilled at working the system and using the syntactical cues of the question to locate the relevant information, copying details from the text without necessarily understanding them. Teachers' exhortations to write answers out in their own words and in full sentences also become a mechanical translating activity where the main points are often not fully grasped.

Real comprehension depends on a well-defined purpose and context for reading. Research evidence also shows that prior knowledge of the subject content of the reading material plays a key role in comprehension and performance on individual comprehension tests has a large task-specific component (DES, 1988). Tests based on a single passage therefore provide a very unreliable guide to the kind of purposeful reading of which children are capable.

One of the earliest ways that pupils can show their grasp of the main ideas of a text is by retelling story or reporting back information they have researched to a partner or a group. Such activities were part of the reading programme described in Chapters 6 and 7 and the teacher of the class made a practice of noting down children's contributions in the feedback sessions, helping her to form a more complete picture of their reading abilities, particularly their ability to draw inferences. Some reading tasks were also based on curriculum purposes for finding and collating information for project work.

Reading assessment and the National Curriculum

The nature of the tests prescribed by the National Curriculum is fraught with contradictions because of the many different purposes they are meant to serve. Not only are they intended to be part of a formative assessment, monitoring individual progress against particular criteria, but they are also intended to give a global picture of the standards of attainment of a particular cohort, plotting performance over time. The contradictions inherent in these intentions can be seen in the different provisions already made for testing at ages 7 and 14 years.

The Standard Assessment Tasks in reading for Key Stage 1 (age 7) are currently largely based on children's ability to read familiar narratives, taken from a prescribed list, while the teacher records the number and the nature of the errors made and ascribes a reading level in relation to the number of words adequately read. This is followed by an oral questioning stage where the reader is asked questions about the story. For example, the 1992 instructions for assessment at Level 3 asked the teacher to use questions such as:

- How do you think that happened?
- How do you think she felt when that happened?
- Can you think of other stories like this one?
- What sort of person was that?
- What part of a story was that?

The teacher assessing looks for evidence that the child:

- understands at least two points requiring the use of inference and deduction;
- refers to the beginning, the development or middle of the story, not merely brief responses to the teacher's questions.

In addition, the teacher is asked to assess children's use of reference material:

- In the course of topic or other work ask the child to find a book or magazine on the subject being researched by using the class or school library classification system.
- Ask the children to search read for at least two pieces of information on their chosen topic.

STORIES OF READING

Stories can be told about all kinds of happenings especially if they have developed over a period of time.

Write the story of how you learned to read and the reading you do now. It will help your teacher find out about the kinds of books you enjoy reading and the sort of reading you did in your last school.

MY
READING
STORY

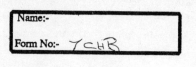

Name:-

Form No:- YCHB

LEARNING TO READ.

Who taught you? Did you find it easy or hard? Can you remember any of your first books?

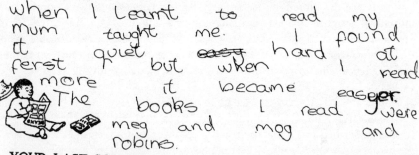

when I learnt to read my mum taught me. I found it ferst quiet but when ~~easy~~ hard at ferst more it became easyer. The books I read were meg and mog and robins.

YOUR LAST SCHOOL

What did you like to read? What didn't you enjoy? Which books did your teacher read to you?

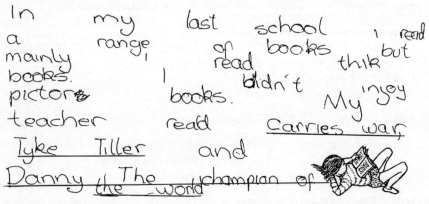

In my last school I read a range of books thik but mainly read books. I pictor books. didn't My injoy teacher read carries war, Tyke Tiller and Danny the The champian of world

Figure 8.1 Keith's reading story

FAVOURITE BOOKS
Why do you think you like them? Do you share books with anyone else?

I liked because Carries
war exsiting because its
she gets evacuated to the
contry side.

COMICS AND MAGAZINES
Which do you buy? Which are your favourite characters? Do you have a hobby or interest that you like to read about?

The comics i buy are
the Beno and
Dandy. I allso buy the
match football magazine, because

TIME AND PLACE
Where and when do you enjoy reading? Do you like reading out loud?
it has posters and facs

I like reading in
quiet places and outdoors
I dont like reading outloud

SELECTION
Where do you get your books from and how do you choose them?
I get
my books from
W. H. smits. I chouse
books by redding the
back cover or the
introduction

COMMENTS
What do parents, teachers and friends say to you about your reading?
my parents think im a
good reader and my
other teachers have said that
too.

How would you complete the following? *READING IS.......F.U.N......*

Figure 8.1

Although these activities are time consuming as a method of testing a whole year group on a single occasion, they are closely related to formative assessment of reading in the classroom and something teachers can be working on throughout the key stage. However, in 1992, teachers could also choose to administer a booklet of reading comprehension items. This booklet contained several different kinds of reading activity such as matching captions to pictures, sentence completion on the context of a complete passage, taking information from a chart and comprehension of a short piece of narrative. These tasks were optional but had to be administered to a whole group at particular times rather than at a child's own pace. Such tests are very unlike the work our youngest children experience as part of the learning process and are based on a very narrow view of reading. In fact, one of the test materials was a collection of *Aesop's Fables*, a genre of writing with which my own research had shown children to be least familiar.

Similarly, in the 1993 pilot tasks for Key Stage 2, a booklet of reading comprehension tasks was provided, with an emphasis on short written outcomes, in some cases through multiple-choice questions on a short story. The reading tests set for Key Stage 3 (14-year olds), in 1993 asked almost exclusively for short written answers. Questions were set on a prescribed anthology of reading, additional to the school's chosen curriculum, as well as a paper based on cloze procedures, whose deletions were designed to test the reader's knowledge about language, particularly grammatical 'correctness'. Such tests, completed in examination conditions with strict time limits have little to do with the process of teaching and learning and are intended ultimately to provide data for league tables of school performance. They place undue emphasis on the ability to write quickly and succinctly and take no account of more considered responses that build over time. There are other problems associated with the way in which the results of the tests have to be reported as a single level of attainment, in that each level covers such a wide spectrum of ability that it is difficult to make generalizations about standards in a particular area of attainment.

Reading standards

It is clearly important for educationalists and politicians to be able to see whether standards of literacy in a particular population of children are rising or falling. Part of the difficulty in identifying the general picture of differential levels reading attainment at the current time is lack of commonalty amongst local education authorities in the kind of data they have collected and the outdated nature of some of the items in the standard reading tests employed. The problem has not yet been solved by the Standard Assessment Tests of the National Curriculum because yearly variations in the methods of testing, as well as constant changes to the actual orders, have made comparisons between performance in different years unreliable. The refusal of teachers to test children in 1993 also lessens the likelihood of useful comparisons being made available.

The most comprehensive picture to date of pupil's reading abilities has been provided by the Assessment and Performance Unit (APU). From 1975 to 1983, following the Bullock Report, the English team developed tests for sampling the school population's attainments in the language curriculum at ages 11 and 15. In each survey, a series of test booklets which contained readings that were thematically related were used. The booklets generally included a page of contents, an index and other cues such as page or chapter headings. Pupils were often gradually exposed to information of greater detail and complexity; some questions were devised which required pupils to integrate information derived from different sections of the booklets. Attempts were also made to obtain different kinds of response by asking pupils to complete forms, fill in tables, label diagrams and design posters. The questions aimed to be similar to those that an experienced teacher would be likely to ask pupils taking account of the subject matter, the form and the function of the reading material.

The material included works of reference, works of literature and reading materials used for practical purposes in everyday life. The design was such that any one pupil completed only one or two tests out of the total range but large enough samples were used to get a broad picture. Some identical tests were used in the 1979 and 1983 surveys and a measure of average test facility was used to make comparisons. The APU was able to make comments on such matters as the relative performance of boys and girls and the differences in attitude and preferences (DES, 1988). The methods are time consuming but the use of sampling ensures that the learning whole cohorts of children are not disturbed and more complex data can be collected.

I began this chapter by suggesting that teachers need to decide what purpose the assessment of reading has in terms of teaching and learning. It is equally important to make national decisions about how the assessment of reading can help inform all concerned with education about where attention is most urgently required to maintain high standards and then take action to provide adequate resources and support for good practice. The small research survey I conducted revealed very little that has not been reported before: boys' relative lack of interest in fiction when compared with girls' reading at the same age; a lack of structured reading provision after the early stages of learning to read; a comparative neglect of reading for information; a general lack of direction in selecting fiction in the middle years. What schools require are not more methods of testing but adequate resources in terms of library and book provision and sufficient curriculum time to develop what everyone agrees is the most important basic tool of learning, no matter what the format of the text or whether the source of the text is a computer screen or a thousand-year-old document.

Conclusions

1 The assessment of reading in schools needs to be planned as an integral part of the teaching and learning processes and should make a positive contribution to learning.

2 Day-to-day opportunities for assessment are provided whenever the teacher:
   (i) organizes group or class discussion of texts and reading tasks;
   (ii) provides reading activities which ask for inferential and evaluative responses (DARTs);
   (iii) uses a text as a model for pupils' own writing;
   (iv) discusses the choice of reading with individuals;
   (v) provides an opportunity for reading aloud to the class, in pairs or groups, from plays and poems, as well as the children's own work;
   (vi) organizes research on a class topic involving note taking and reporting;
   (vii) hears an individual read, noting the strategies used for making meaning in a running record, miscue analysis or informal reading inventory;
   (viii) uses a cloze procedure to develop understanding of a particular text or textual feature.

3 Children should know on what criteria they are being assessed and be given a role in the record-keeping process. ·

4 Parents can make a positive contribution to the overall picture of their children's reading development and their comments and views should be invited. These can be recorded in shared comment books or as part of a more detailed reading record such as *The Primary Language Record* (Barrs *et al.*, 1988).

5 The danger of an imposed procedure of testing, which concentrates on what is easily assessed, is that it limits teacher's aspirations and begins to determine what is taught. Teaching to the test works to narrow and restrict the curriculum.

6 The purpose of assessment should not be to expose what children cannot do but to identify ways of helping each individual to develop from where they are and to provide safe challenges which stretch children's abilities towards targets within their grasp.

7 Portfolios of work including children's and parents' records of reading can be kept in the same way as portfolios of writing. They can provide details of range and breadth of reading interest and attitudes to reading. They will also provide the basis for reports to parents and other teachers at appropriate times in the school year.

8 More formally organized records of children's stages of learning, on the model of the *Primary Language Record*, form a very useful document for transfer between classes and schools.

9 Children with reading difficulties should be helped through assessment to identify the strategies they already use for dealing with unknown words and to extend their word attack skills.

10 Bi-literate pupils need to feel that the reading and writing they do in their community languages is valued. They should be encouraged to talk about their experience and this should be recorded in order to create a full picture of their abilities.

11 Sampling populations at regular intervals by a range of reading tasks is a more effective way of monitoring reading standards than is provided by assessment procedures linked to the National Curriculum.

References

Appleyard, J.A. (1990) *Becoming a Reader*, Cambridge: Cambridge University Press.

Assessment of Performance Unit (APU) (1987) *Language Performance in Schools, Review of APU Language Monitoring 1979–83 Assessment Matters: No. 4*, London: HMSO.

Barrs, M. and Thomas, A. (eds) (1991) *The Reading Book*, London: Centre for Language in Primary Education/London Borough of Southwark.

Barrs, M., Ellis, S., Hester, H. and Thomas, A. (1988) *The Primary Language Record: A Handbook for Teachers*, London: Centre for Language in Primary Education/ Inner London Education Authority.

Barthes, R. (1974) *S/Z: An Essay* (trans. R. Miller), New York: Hill and Wang, London: Collins, Fontana Press.

Barthes, R. (1977) *Image Music Text* (trans. S. Heath), London: Fontana Press.

Beard, R. (1987) *Developing Reading 3–13*, London: Hodder and Stoughton.

Bennett, J. (1982) *Learning to Read with Picture Books*, Stroud, Thimble Press.

Boyce, E.R. (1977) Gay Way Introductory Series.

Britton, J. (1977) The nature of the reader's satisfactions. In M. Meek, A. Warlow and G. Barton (eds) *The Cool Web*, London: Bodley Head.

Carter, R. (1990) *Knowledge about Language and the Curriculum*, London: Hodder and Stoughton.

Clark, M. (1976) *Young Fluent Readers*, Oxford: Heinemann Educational.

Clay, M. (1979) *Reading: The Patterning of Complex Behaviour*, Auckland, London: Heinemann Educational.

Connell, M. (1985) 'An experiment in reader response and some implications for the teaching of literature', Dissertation for MEd, Sheffield University.

Culler, J. (1981) *The Pursuit of Signs, Semiotics, Literature, Deconstruction*, London: Routledge and Kegan Paul.

Davies, F. (1986) The function of the text book in sciences and the humanities. In B. Gilham (ed.) *The Language of School Subjects*, London: Heinemann.

Delamont, S. (1990) *Sex Roles and the School*, London: Routledge.

DES (1975) *A Language for Life*. Report of the Committee of Inquiry appointed by the Secretary of State for Education and Science under the Chairmanship of Sir Alan Bullock, London: HMSO.

DES (1988) *Language Performance in Schools: Review of APU Language Monitoring 1979–1983*, London: HMSO.

DES (1989) *English for Ages 5 to 16* (The Cox Report), London: HMSO.

DES (1991) *The Implementation of the Curricular Requirements of the Education Reform Act: English, Key Stage 1*, London: HMSO.

DFE (Department for Education) (1993) *English for Ages 5 to 16, Proposals of the Secretary of State for Education*, London: HMSO.

Dombey, H. (1992) *Words and Worlds: Reading in the Early Years of School*, Sheffield: National Association for the Teaching of English Publications.

Donaldson, M (1993) Sense and sensibility: some thoughts on the teaching of literacy. In R. Beard (ed.) *Teaching Literacy Balancing Perspectives*, London: Hodder and Stoughton.

Eagleton, T. (1983) *Literary Theory; An Introduction*, Oxford: Blackwell.

English and Media Centre (1984a) *Making Stories*, London: Inner London Education Authority.

English and Media Centre (1984b) *Changing Stories*, London: Inner London Education Authority.

Fish, S. (1980) *Is There a Text in this Class? The Authority of Interpretive Communities*, Cambridge, MA: Harvard University Press.

Fisher, M. (1970) Is fiction educational?. In *Children's Literature in Education*, Vol. 1, March 1970, pp. 11–20.

Fry, D. (1985) *Children Talk About Books: Seeing Themselves as Readers*, Milton Keynes: Open University Press.

Goodman, K.S. (1982) The Goodman model of reading. In F.V. Gollasch (ed.) *Language and Literacy, The Selected Writings of Kenneth S. Goodman, Vol. 1*, London: Routledge and Kegan Paul.

Gorman, T. and Kispal, A. (1987) *Pupil's Attitudes to Reading*. Windsor: NFER/Nelson for the Assessment of Performance Unit.

Graves, D. (1983) *Writing: Teachers and Children at Work*, London: Heinemann.

Griffiths, P. (1991) *English at the Core: Dialogue and Power in English Teaching*, Buckingham: Open University Press.

Hall, N. (1987) *The Emergence of Literacy*, London: Hodder and Stoughton.

Hannon, P. (1990) Parental involvement in pre-school literacy development. In D. Wray (ed.) *Emerging Partnerships: Current Research in Language and Literacy (BERA Dialogues 4)*, Clevedon: Multilingual Matters.

Hardy, B. (1975) *Tellers and Listeners the Narrative Imagination*. Dover, NH: Longwood; London: Athlone Press.

Hasan, R. (1980) The texture of a text. In *Sophia Linguistic Working Papers in Linguistics VI*, Tokyo: The Graduate School of Languages and Linguistics, pp. 43–90.

Hayhoe, M. and Parker, S. (eds) (1990) *Reading and Response*, Milton Keynes: Open University Press.

Heath, S.B. (1983) *Ways with Words: Language, Life and Work in Communities and Classrooms*, Cambridge: Cambridge University Press.

Holdaway, D. (1979) *The Foundations of Literacy*, New York: Aston Scholastic.

Hughes, T. (1963) *How the Whale Became*, London: Faber.

Iser, W. (1978) *The Act of Reading: A Theory of Aesthetic Response*, Baltimore, MD: Johns Hopkins University Press; London: Routledge and Kegan Paul.

Ivanic, R. and Hamilton, H. (1990) Literacy beyond school. In D. Wray (ed.) *BERA Dialogues: Emerging Partnerships: Current Research in Language and Literacy*, Clevedon: Multilingual Matters.

Leeson, R. (1985) *Reading and Righting: The Past, Present and Future of Fiction for the Young*, London: Collins.

Leggett, J., O'Connor, M. and Scott, A. (eds) (1989) *The 'M' File*, London: Macmillan Education.

Littlefair, A.B. (1991) *Reading All Types of Writing: The Importance of Genre and Register for Reading Development*, Milton Keynes: Open University Press.

Lunzer, A. and Gardner, K. (1979) *The Effective Use of Reading*, London: Heinemann Educational.

Mark, J. (1976) *Thunder and Lightnings*. Harmondsworth: Puffin.

Martin, J.R. (1989) *Factual Writing: Exploring and Challenging Social Reality*, Oxford: Oxford University Press.

McNally, J. and Murray, W. (1968) *Key Words to Literacy (2nd edition)*, London: The Schoolmaster Publishing Company.

Meek, M. (1982) *Learning to Read*, London: Bodley Head.

Meek, M. (1993) *Achieving Literacy*, London: Routledge and Kegan Paul.

Meek, M. (1988) *How Texts Teach What Readers Learn*, Stroud: Thimble Press.

Meek, M. (1990). What do we know about reading that helps us teach? In R. Carter (ed.) *Knowledge About Language and the Curriculum, The LINC Reader*. London: Hodder and Stoughton.

Meek, M. (1991) *On Being Literate*, London: Bodley Head.

Meek, M. (1992a) Literacy, redescribing reading. In K. Kimberley, M. M. and J. Miller (eds) *New Readings: Contributions to an Understanding of Literacy*, London: A. & C. Black.

Meek, M. (1992b) Children reading – now. In Styles, M., Bearne, E. and Watson, V. (eds), *After Alice*, Fakenham, Norfolk: Cassell, pp. 172–89.

Millard, E. (1985) Stories to grow on. In *Alice in Genderland*, Sheffield: National Association for the Teaching of English Publications.

Millard, E. (1988) The tyranny of tastes. In *English 'A' Level in Practice*, Sheffield: National Association for the Teaching of English Publications.

Minns, H. (1989) *Read It To Me Now*, London: Virago.

Minns, H. (1991) *Language Literacy and Gender*, Sevenoaks: Hodder and Stoughton.

Moon, C. (1980) *Individualised Reading*, University of Reading: Centre for the Teaching of Reading.

Moss, G. (1989) *Unpopular Fictions*, London: Virago.

Neate, B. (1992) *Finding Out About Finding Out. A Practical Guide to Children's Information Books*, Bury St Edmunds: Hodder and Stoughton in association with the United Kingdom Reading Association.

Nelms, B. and Zancanella, D. (1990) The experience and study of literature. In M. Hayhoe and S. Parker (eds) *Reading and Response*, Milton Keynes: Open University Press.

Nottinghamshire Advisory and Inspection Service and Educational Psychology Service (1991) *Teaching Reading in Nottinghamshire Primary Schools Report, No. 18/91*, Nottingham: Nottinghamshire County Council Education.

Ousbey, J. (1992) Reading and the imagination. In C. Harrison and M. Coles (eds) *The Reading for Real Handbook*, London: Routledge.

Paley, V.P. (1984) *Boys and Girls: Superheroes in the Doll Corner*. Chicago, IL: University of Chicago, pp. 203–4.

Perera, K. (1993) The good book: linguistic aspects. In R. Beard (ed.) *Teaching Literacy Balancing Perspectives*, London: Hodder and Stoughton.

Protherough, R. (1983) *Developing Response to Fiction*, Milton Keynes: Open University Press.

Protherough, R. (1987) The stories that readers tell. In B. Corcoran, and E. Evans, (eds) *Readers, Texts, Teachers*, Milton Keynes: Open University Press.

Protherough, R. (1990) Children's recognition of stories. In M. Hayhoe and S. Parker (eds) *Reading and Response*, Milton Keynes: Open University Press.

Pumfrey, P. (1991) *Improving Children's Reading in the Junior School: Challenges and Responses*, London: Cassell.

Riddell, S. (1989) Resistance and gender codes. In *Gender and Education*, Vol. 1, No. 2.

Sadler, M. (1986) *Alistair's Time Machine*, London: Macmillan, Picturemac.

Sarland, C. (1990) *Young People Reading: Culture and Response*. Milton Keynes: Open University Press.

Sarland, C. (1991) *Young People Reading: Culture and Response*, Milton Keynes: Open University Press.

Sendak, M. (1970) *Where the Wild Things Are*. Harmondsworth: Puffin Books.

Schonnell, F.J. (1945) *The Psychology and Teaching of Reading*, Edinburgh and London: Oliver and Boyd.

Sheeran, Y. and Barnes, D. (1991) *Writing in Schools*, Milton Keynes: Open University Press.

Smith, F. (1984) *Reading that Helps us Teach, Joining the Literacy Club*, Reading: Reading Reading Centre.

Smith, F. (1992) Reading the bear facts. In *English in Education*, Vol. 26, No. 1, Spring, pp. 17–25.

Southgate, V., Arnold, H. and Johnston, S. (1981) *Extending Beginning Reading*, London: Heinemann.

Stibbs, A. (1991) *Reading Narrative as Literature: Signs of Life*, Milton Keynes: Open University Press.

Taylor, M. (1991) Books in the classroom and knowledge about language. In R. Carter (ed.) *Knowledge about Language, and the Curriculum*, London: Hodder and Stoughton.

Temple, C., Nathan, R., Burris, N. and Temple, F. (1988) *The Beginnings of Writing*, Newton, MA: Allyn and Bacon.

Wade, B. (1990) *Reading for Real*, Milton Keynes: Open University Press.

Warwick University (1992) *English at Key Stages 1, 2 and 3. Second Interim Report to the NCC*.

Waterland, L. (1985) *Read with Me: An Apprenticeship Approach to Reading*, Stroud: Thimble Press.

Weinberger, J., Hannon, P. and Nutbrown, C. (1990) *Ways of Working with Parents to Promote early literacy development*. Sheffield: Sheffield University, Division of Education.

Wells, G. (1985) *Language, Learning and Education: Selected Papers from the Bristol Study 'Language at Home and at School'*, Windsor: NFER/Nelson.

West, A. (1986) The production of readers. In *The English Magazine: Literature*, No. 17, Autumn, pp. 4–22.

White, J. (1990) On literacy and gender. In R. Carter (ed.) *Knowledge About Language and the Curriculum*, London: Hodder and Stoughton, pp. 181–97.

Whitehead, F. (1966) *The Disappearing Dais, A Study of the Principles and Practice of English Teaching*, London: Chatto and Windus.

Whitehead, F., Capey, A.C. and Maddren, W. (1974) *Children's Reading Interests*, London: Schools Council/Methuen.

Whitehead, F., Capey, A.C., Maddren, W. and Wellings, A. (1977) *Children and their Books*, London: Macmillan.

Willinsky, J. and Hunniford, M. (1993) Reading the romance younger: the mirrors and fears of a preparatory literacy. In L. Christian-Smith, (ed.) *Texts of Desire*, London, Washington: Falmer Press.

Wilson, D.H. (1986) *There's a Wolf in My Pudding; Twelve Twisted and Tortured, Grim and Gruesome, Tall and Terrible Tales*, London: Macmillan, Papermac.

Index